A Girl's Guide to Buying Diamonds

A Girl's Guide to Buying Diamonds

How to Choose, Evaluate, and Buy the Diamond You Want

RANDI MOLOFSKY

GLOUCESTER MASSACHUSETTS

QUARRY BOOKS

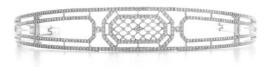

First published in the United States of America by
Quarry Books, a member of
Quayside Publishing Group
33 Commercial Street
Gloucester, Massachusetts 01930-5089
Telephone: (978) 282-9590
Fax: (978) 283-2742
www.rockpub.com

Library of Congress Cataloging-in-Publication Data
Molofsky, Randi.
    A girl's guide to buying diamonds : how to choose,
    evaluate, and buy the diamond you want / Randi Molofsky.
        p. cm.
    ISBN 1-59253-174-1 (pbk.)
    1. Diamonds—Purchasing.   I. Title.
TS753.M65 2005
736'.23—dc22   2005008065
                                                        CIP

ISBN 1-59253-174-1

10 9 8 7 6 5 4 3 2 1

Design: Dutton & Sherman Design
Cover Image: Richard Pierce/Courtesy of Tiffany & Co.

Printed in Singapore

This book is dedicated to Mrs. Forrester, Mrs. Brennan, and Dr. W. for English 101; and to Mom and Dad for their tireless support of a struggling writer.

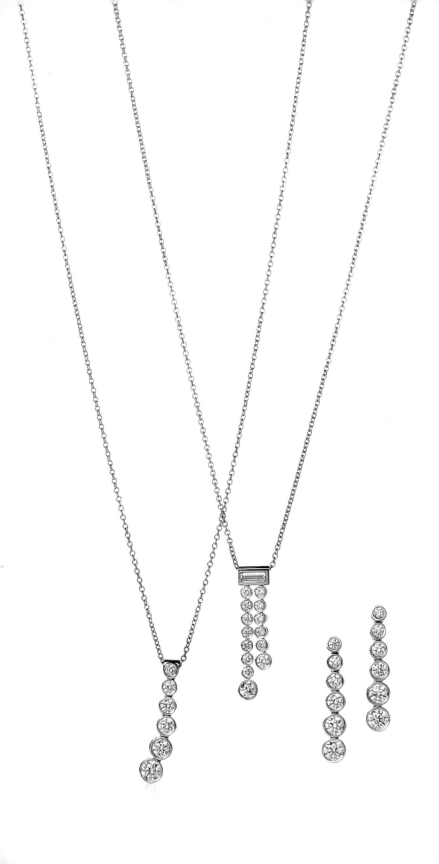

CONTENTS

PREFACE

THIS BOOK IS FOR those women who know what they want and are not afraid to go for it. Whether you are a cutthroat trial lawyer or a noted painter, you have harnessed your dreams and have made them a reality. You know that women can accomplish anything they set their minds to, and they'll do it with style.

Whether you have an impressive jewelry wardrobe or are just beginning to accumulate a collection, this book allows women to throw away the old conceptions that diamonds designate betrothal or celebrity. You don't need a marriage proposal or a million dollars to own diamonds, and the next five chapters will give you the tools and knowledge to make purchases stress-free.

By following the tips in this book, you will get not only an idea of what kind of diamonds you should buy, but also how to build your jewelry wardrobe in a way that complements your personality and your lifestyle.

Be aware: This book isn't a quick reference for getting the cheapest stones, but a tool that will help you buy diamond jewelry that will not only be enjoyed today, but will be an heirloom for generations to come. From the basic facts to more specific topics, such as vintage jewels and the newest red-carpet trends, this book will give you the confidence to walk into a store and ask the right questions to make an informed purchase.

Without a doubt, jewelry is fun and empowering. There is no shame in feeling beautiful, and the most successful women know how to combine beauty, confidence and intellectual prowess to make things happen. Hopefully, by the end of this book, you will want to let yourself shine—via personality and accessories!

DIAMONDS ARE A GIRL'S BEST FRIEND

Gentlemen Prefer Blondes: It was the movie that spawned the catchphrase that has haunted men for more than a half-century. Marilyn Monroe and Jane Russell were two "little girls from Little Rock" taking a transatlantic cruise to Paris, and meeting men along the way. Every self-respecting diamond lover should know the lyrics to this classic movie tune.

DIAMONDS ARE A GIRL'S BEST FRIEND
Music by Jules Styne / Lyrics by Leo Robin

The French were bred to die for love
they delight in fighting duels
but I prefer a man who lives
and gives expensive jewels.

A kiss on the hand may be quite Continental
but diamonds are a girl's best friend.
A kiss may be grand but it won't pay the rental
on your humble flat, or help you at the automat.
Men grow cold as girls grow old
and we all lose our charms in the end.
But square-cut or pear-shaped
these rocks don't lose their shape
Diamonds are a girl's best friend
. . . Tiffany's . . . Cartier . . .
Talk to me, Harry Winston, tell me all about it!

There may come a time when a lass needs a lawyer
but diamonds are a girl's best friend.
There may come a time when a hard-boiled employer
thinks you're awful nice
but get that ice or else no dice.
He's your guy when stocks are high
but beware when they start to descend,
It's then that those louses go back to their spouses
Diamonds are a girl's best friend.

I've heard of affairs that are strictly platonic
but diamonds are a girl's best friend,
and I think affairs that you must keep liaisonic
are better bets if little pets get big baguettes.
Time rolls on and youth is gone
and you can't straighten up when you bend
but stiff back or stiff knees
you stand straight at Tiffany's
Diamonds . . . Diamonds . . .
—I don't mean rhinestones—
but diamonds are a girl's best friend.

INTRODUCTION

A Tale of Empowerment (or Why I Love Diamonds)

I HAVE LOVED ACCESSORIES ever since I learned to dress myself. Besides the topic at hand—diamonds—I have forever cherished handbags. I adore shoes ranging from pumps to mules to stilettos, and my sunglasses have run the gamut from aviators to vintage plastic shades. My favorite anecdote comes from my mother who tells me that at about age five, I spent an entire year refusing to leave the house without wearing a belt with every outfit I chose. In fact, there are pictures of me posing on the beach that summer wearing a very lovely cotton belt with my one-piece blue suit.

Like most young girls, I spotted my first diamond on my mom's left hand. The round stone set in yellow gold piqued my interest and I, like many little girls, have played "make believe" with not only that ring, but with various dime-store versions of the simple solitaire.

In recent years, I have had the definite pleasure of searching the globe for fabulous jewelry trends. I have tried on the very same 20-plus carat diamond that entertainer Jennifer Lopez wore to a recent Academy Awards ceremony. Marquise-shaped and set horizontally in a ring, the Harry Winston piece stretched across three of my fingers. I have personally chosen cascading diamond chandeliers and enormous briolette necklaces to be loaned out to the likes of Nicole Kidman and Queen Latifah. (And yes, I modeled each and every piece in front of a mirror myself before loaning it out.) The moral of this story: Seeing yourself in fabulous diamonds never gets old.

Here's where this book comes into play. For too many years, diamonds have traditionally been seen only as a gift from a man to a woman on ultraspecial occasions, such as an engagement or anniversary. Luckily, ladies, the times they are a-changing. Fueled by the buying power and style savvy of successful women in the twenty-first century, buying diamonds today has no restrictions. Dying for a pair of simple studs? Want to treat yourself to a tennis bracelet? Found a diamond ring that you adore but you have no intention of getting married anytime soon? Feel empowered to make the purchase yourself.

Even if you've never thought to buy fancy jewels for yourself in the past, this book will give you all the insight and technical information you need to make an informed purchase. From the Four C's (cut, clarity, color, and carat) to buying the right pieces for your unique personality, all the tips and tricks of the trade are now at your fingertips.

And, if you're still not convinced that diamonds may be your best purchase ever, here is my top-ten list of diamond pros:

10 ♦ Diamonds will not talk back to you.
9 ♦ Diamonds don't have fat, calories, or carbs.
8 ♦ Unlike "man's best friend," diamonds won't shed on your new black sweater.
7 ♦ Diamonds won't be late to dinner.
6 ♦ Diamonds won't hog the remote control.
5 ♦ Diamonds don't need electricity, gas, or a motor to make them run.
4 ♦ Diamonds won't tell you lies or make excuses.
3 ♦ Diamonds won't make you break out.
2 ♦ Diamonds are in season all year long.

And finally…

1 ♦ Diamonds will never go out of style.

Happy diamond shopping!

CHAPTER ONE

Diamond Basics

BETTER A DIAMOND WITH A FLAW
THAN A PEBBLE WITHOUT.

—*Confucius*

I F YOU PICKED UP THIS BOOK, there is one fact already established: you love diamonds. Maybe you own one, or a few, or maybe you aspire to make a purchase one day soon. It seems clichéd to say that most women covet diamonds, but let's face it, the act of adorning oneself with a glittering diamond bauble is often enough to inspire ear-to-ear grins, oohs and aahs, and countless compliments from friends. Do you remember when you first fell under the spell of diamonds? It could have been when you gazed upon your mother's engagement ring as a child, or maybe when you first visited your local jewelry store and peered into the brightly lit glass cases.

Whatever the origin of your diamond devotion, just the act of picking up this book means that you understand that all good shoppers are educated shoppers. Buying precious gemstones should be met with careful consideration and as much knowledge as you can acquire. Because you are a savvy, modern woman, you already understand that there is no need to wait for your diamonds to arrive as a gift. Whether you are saving up for a pair of great solitaire earrings or have made the split-second decision to spend your bonus check on a right-hand diamond ring, your goal should be to own a piece that you will love today, tomorrow, indefinitely—and will have hopes of passing down to future generations.

Chapter one is a great beginning to fulfilling your diamond dreams. It will explore the "Four C's" including Cut, Clarity, Color, and Carat weight. Specifically, you'll become familiar with the most popular diamond cuts through images and descriptions. The system of color and clarity grading will be explained so you can enter any jewelry store and sound like an expert. Next, we'll delve into the world of colored diamonds as you learn just how rare and expensive certain stones can be. You'll discover the origins of diamonds and where they are currently mined. The concepts of synthetic and enhanced diamonds will be explained along with recent legislation devised to combat "blood diamonds," also known as conflict diamonds. Finally, and maybe most importantly, you will learn about the grading report, a document you should get with every diamond purchase, which proves its authenticity and describes its characteristics.

Don't be put off by the prospect of all this studying. Just remember that your payoff purchase will make it completely worthwhile. Gemology is a science all to itself, so don't expect to be an expert, but know that you will soon have the tools to make an informed purchase. Armed with your *Guide*, you'll be ready to hit the stores in no time.

ALL ABOUT CUTS

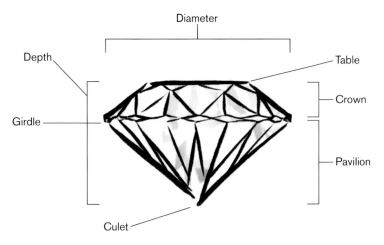

Diamond Anatomy

If diamonds are all about the sparkle, then a great cut should be your first priority when shopping for the newest addition to your jewelry wardrobe. The cut of the stone is actually the means to creating the fire (reflection of rainbow colors) and brilliance (reflection of white light) that occurs when light hits a diamond. When you are inspecting a diamond's cut, it's really about the stone's proportions and uniformity. The more proportionate and uniform the diamond, the better sparkle you'll get.

Let's look at some key factors you'll need to understand when assessing a diamond's cut:

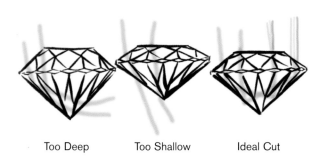

Too Deep   Too Shallow   Ideal Cut

DEPTH AND WIDTH ♦ These two measurements have an enormous impact on the brilliance you will get from your diamond. Light enters the stone from the top, and if it is cut too shallow, light is lost out of the bottom of the stone. If it is cut too deep, the light bounces out of the sides of the stone. When ideal, or evenly cut, the light properly bounces back out of the top of the stone and directly to the eye, creating that famous diamond sparkle.

SYMMETRY ♦ The symmetry of a diamond is created when a stonecutter cuts facets into a rough stone. Every smooth, flat, polished surface on a diamond is called a facet. The more symmetrical and well placed these facets are, the more *scintillation* you'll achieve. Scintillation is the flash you get when light bounces between the facets on your stone.

POLISH ♦ A clean diamond is a happy diamond. As the light moving through a diamond is what makes it sparkle, you don't want anything standing in the way of the light bouncing out of your stone. The polish grade, ranging from excellent to poor, shows how well the cutter brought out the shine in a particular stone.

While these terms might seem technical, a lot of these factors can be assessed with the naked eye. When you're looking at a loose diamond (one that is not set in metal or jewelry) pick it up with a pair of tweezers and view it from the side. Do you see any chips? Does anything look off-center? Is anything sloping or angled to one side? When you look at a group of stones together, which one is the most eye-catching and beautiful? That is probably the diamond with the best cut. Your best bet, especially when shopping for loose stones, is to look at as many diamonds as possible to find the one that makes the most of available light.

DIAMOND SHAPES

You might know a little about which diamond shapes you like. Maybe you prefer a circular look, or maybe rectangular. In today's market, there are quite a few shapes to get to know, and sometimes there are only minor differences between them. The most important thing to know about shapes is that some reflect more light than others, and so they are inherently more brilliant. Additionally, shapes other than the standard round brilliant are referred to as fancy shapes. Again, the more you comparison shop, the more you'll get to know your taste and style when it comes to shape.

Let's take a look at some of the most well-known and popular diamond shapes:

BRILLIANT ◆ This cut is the most popular choice for solitaires because it reflects the most light, giving it more sparkle than all the other cuts. This cut is commonly referred to as *round*. Brilliant-cut stones have fifty-six facets: thirty-two facets above the girdle, and twenty-four below.

Brilliant

PRINCESS ◆ A square cut; the princess is a relatively new cut that has a modern, clean look to it. The extra faceting on the outer corners gives it good sparkle.

Princess

EMERALD ♦ A rectangular cut with truncated corners; there are fewer facets in an emerald shape than in others, which render it less brilliant. This cut does, however, have a classy, elegant look that works well with larger stones.

Emerald

RADIANT ♦ Another rectangular cut, the radiant has added sparkle because of the many facets that are cut into the underside of the stone.

Radiant

OVAL ♦ While the name speaks for itself, oval shapes are for the woman who wants something a little different. After losing popularity for a while, ovals are back for those who like the look of a round stone but crave uniqueness.

Oval

MARQUISE ♦ Another shape that is rebounding in popularity, a marquise diamond is an elliptical shape with two pointed ends. When cut just right, a marquise shape can actually make your diamond look bigger than it is.

Marquise

PEAR ♦ Shaped like a teardrop, a pear shape gives the fire of a brilliant shape without looking conventional.

Pear

HEART ♦ A fancy shape that some find a little too cloying, but others maintain is totally romantic. Be aware that heart shapes don't tend to sparkle as much as other shapes.

Heart

TRILLION ♦ Often used to flank the center stone of a three-stone ring, a trillion is a triangular-shaped cut.

Trillion

BAGUETTE ♦ Another shape used for flanking center stones, baguettes are also often channel set (see chapter two, page 37) next to each other in bracelets.

Baguette

OLD MINE (CUSHION) ◆ One of the first diamond shapes created, this shape has fifty-eight facets, like a modern brilliant cut, but the proportions are different. Square shaped with slightly rounded sides, this shape appeals to those wanting a vintage look. The Hope diamond is old-mine cut.

Old Mine

ASSCHER ◆ The inspiration for the emerald shape, the Asscher was created in the late 1800s. It is a step cut, and when looking into an Asscher, you actually see the levels of "steps" descending into the stone. It makes diamonds look smaller, so this shape is better for larger stones.

Asscher

ROSE ◆ Believed to have been developed in the 1500s in India, the rose cut is faceted on top and flat on the bottom. While it doesn't give off a lot of light, its symmetry and broad facets have given the cut a renaissance in popularity.

Rose

So, how do you go about choosing which shape you want? It's truly all about personal preference. Look to Chapter Two, Settings and Styles for Your Personality, for more information about what shape might be the best fit for you. (Refer to "What Is Your Jewel Tone?" on page 56.)

COLOR

A diamond acts as a prism that divides light into colors. The resulting fire comes from how little or how much color is in a stone. To begin discussing color, you first need to understand that there are both "colorless" diamonds and "fancy colored" diamonds. Colorless diamonds are the traditional white stones seen in most jewelry. These diamonds disperse light throughout the entire stone. The more yellow a diamond is, the more the light is diminished. Here's an easy scheme to help understand diamond color:

Less color = more fire = higher color grade = greater value

The Gemological Institute of America (GIA) created an internationally recognized color-grading system that is ranked alphabetically from D to Z (though the letters T through Y are omitted). D stones are totally colorless, while a Z classification is reserved for fancy colors. If you are looking to buy a diamond that looks white to the naked eye, keep your purchases above J at all times.

Diamond Color Chart																		
Colorless			Near Colorless				Faint Yellow			Very Light Yellow				Light Yellow			Fancy Yellow
D	E	F	G	H	I	J	K	L	M	N	O	P	Q	R	S	Z		Z+

The international Diamond Color Grading System developed by GIA.

FANCY COLORED DIAMONDS

Unlike colorless diamonds, fancy colored diamonds can't really be qualified. While more intensity of color usually results in higher value, beauty is truly in the eye of the beholder for these rare and special stones. While the so-called "pure colors" like yellow, pink, and blue used to be universally considered most desirable, there has been an evolution toward appreciation for secondary or modified colors.

Prices for fancy colored diamonds can range from $1,000 per carat (the unit of diamond weight) to $1 million per carat. According to industry standards, there is one colored diamond mined for every 10,000 colorless diamonds. This explains the usual jump in price for a colored diamond versus a colorless one.

Fancy colored diamonds can, for our purposes, be designated into two categories: very rare, meaning that there are only a few hundred in the world in each of the color families; and rare but commercial, meaning that they exist more widely but are still very expensive. Here are the characteristics of fancy colors and what categories they fall into:

VERY RARE

GREEN ♦ Green diamonds are extremely rare and tend to be more pastel in color, although there are a few stones that can approach emerald green's depth. They can have yellow or blue as modifying colors. Green diamonds are known to form in two ways: First by natural irradiation

Green

(meaning they have been sitting in the ground for millions of years next to something radioactive, though the diamonds do not become radioactive). The second is by the inclusion of hydrogen atoms in the pure carbon structure. Colored diamonds are found in South America (Guyana, Brazil and Venezuela), Borneo, and potentially any African country.°

° In theory, any colored diamond can come from any mine in any part of the world where diamonds are mined. There are certain places that have shown a predominance of certain colors, though, such as the African continent.

PURPLE ♦ Purple diamonds are so rare they are considered more of a collector's item. Purple diamonds tend to have a gray or pinkish modifier. They are generally small and less then one carat in size and are included with imperfections. The color in purple diamonds is caused by "graining." Purple diamonds are most often found in Russia.

Purple

VIOLET ♦ Violet diamonds are extremely rare, and because only a handful exist, are considered a collectors' item. They generally have a gray modifier and a dark appearance. Violet diamonds also tend to be small in size, with most stones less than one carat. Their color is caused by hydrogen, and Australia is the major source of violet diamonds.

Violet

ORANGE ♦ Orange diamonds tend to be pastel but are saturated like a pumpkin or carrot on rare occasion. They tend to be modified by yellow or brown, and their color is caused by nitrogen in the pure carbon structure. They are predominantly found in South Africa.

Orange

RED ◆ Red diamonds are very rare, tend to be small in size (less than one carat) and are in essence super-saturated, dark pink diamonds. They are usually modified by purple or brown. Graining is responsible for the red color, and they are predominantly found in Australia, Brazil, and Africa.

Red

RARE BUT COMMERCIAL
(OFTEN CALLED "PURE" DIAMOND COLORS)

YELLOW ◆ Yellow can exist from the fairly common pastel or light shades to the very rare canary. This is the color most commercially available and often the most pleasing. The yellow color in diamonds is caused by nitrogen. Most are found in South Africa, Brazil, and Africa.

Yellow

BROWN ◆ Brown diamonds have the greatest variation of shades and saturations and can be referred to as champagne, chocolate, or cognac. They can be modified by yellow, orange, or green. Their color is caused by graining, and they are found in Australia, Brazil, South Africa, and potentially any African country.

Brown

PINK ◆ Pink diamonds tend to be pastel but on rare occasions can be very saturated. Pink diamonds are often modified by purple, orange, or brown. The color in pink diamonds is caused by graining, and they come from Australia, Brazil, South Africa, India*, Russia, and Africa.

Pink

BLUE ◆ Blue diamonds are very rare and tend to be of a pastel shade, but range to the very rare deep and vivid blues. They are often modified by gray, and rarely by green. They can come in very big sizes (such as the 45.52 carat Hope Diamond). Their color is caused by boron, and blues are primarily found in South Africa, India, and Africa.

Blue

There are also black, white, and gray diamonds. Genuine black diamonds are usually treated with radiation to make their color appear more black. These are the stones found in most black diamond jewelry. There are also "natural" black diamonds that are not treated. These stones have their color as the result of many graphite inclusions. Because of these inclusions, or breaks, untreated black diamonds are difficult to cut and will often fracture. White diamonds have a milky appearance, and gray diamonds can range from pale to dark.

---

* India's diamond mines have been exhausted for hundreds of years, though there is still occasional mining. The Hope diamond was mined there in the seventeenth century.

From the Expert:
What to Know About Colored Diamonds

Alan Bronstein is one of the most trusted names in colored diamonds. His two books, *Collecting and Classifying Colored Diamonds* and *Forever Brilliant: The Aurora Collection of Colored Diamonds* have established him as an expert on the subject. He is also the curator of the world's most famous natural fancy colored diamond collections, the Aurora and the Butterfly of Peace. The Aurora collection is on display at the American Museum of Natural History in New York, while the Butterfly of Peace collection is currently on display at the Smithsonian Institution in Washington, DC.

According to Bronstein, the key to buying a colored diamond relies totally on the buyer's perception of its beauty. He thinks that women should be empowered to choose what they find most beautiful, not most expensive. "Women should feel liberated to choose what they like the best, because they are the ones who are wearing the stone," Bronstein explains. "To say that a saturated color is more beautiful than a pale one is absurd. It's all in the eye of the beholder. Beauty is not based on rarity or monetary value."

While Bronstein does not think that buying from a colored diamond specialist is required, he does suggest working with a dealer who is respected and has knowledge of what he or she is selling. The rarer the stone you are seeking, he advises, the more a specialist would be required. What is required in a colored diamond purchase, as in any other diamond purchase, is certification (see page 37). "You must not be satisfied with just a description or appraisal from the owner," he says. "You need a gemological report to confirm that your stone is truly a natural color and not enhanced in any way."

Most importantly, Bronstein says, remember that appraising colored diamonds is very subjective. When it comes to the rarest stones, there isn't a consensus on their values. The less rare stones can be compared to one another, and therefore their values can be quantified.

CLARITY

Small, internal flaws or cracks in a diamond are called *inclusions*. These little imperfections make all the difference in terms of the value and appearance of your diamond. Clarity grades are based on a scale ranging from FL (Flawless) to I (Imperfect). These grades are international clarity standards. Except for I grade stones, in which inclusions can be seen with the naked eye, the rest of the chart is determined by looking at a stone under 10x magnification.

Here, ranging from highest to lowest quality (least to most heavily included), is the grading scale for diamond clarity:

- ♦ *FL (Flawless)*: There are no internal or external flaws.
- ♦ *IF (Internally Flawless)*: There are no observable internal flaws but some external ones that can be removed.
- ♦ *VVS1 (Very Very Slightly Included 1)*: In these stones, it is very difficult to see inclusions from the top of the stone under 10x magnification.

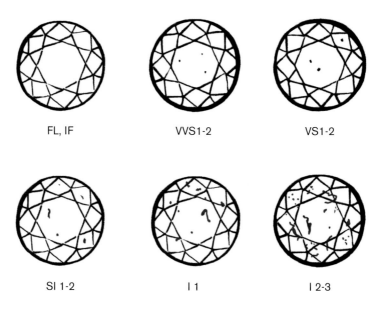

| FL, IF | VVS1-2 | VS1-2 |

| SI 1-2 | I 1 | I 2-3 |

- VVS2 *(Very Very Slightly Included 2)*: In these stones, it is difficult to see inclusions from the bottom of the stone under 10x magnification.
- VS *(Very Slightly Included)*: Flaws can be seen with 10x magnification but are not highly visible.
- SI *(Slightly Included)*: With magnification, it is not hard to spot flaws. Inclusions might be visible with the naked eye.
- I *(Imperfect)*: Inclusions are visible to the naked eye.

When you join together the clarity and color scales, you have a better picture of your diamond's overall value. For example, a D-Flawless stone is the most rare and expensive diamond. It has the highest grade of both color and clarity.

CARAT WEIGHT

In the world of jewelry, there are *carats* and there are *karats*. When you're talking about diamonds, the "c" version of the word is in reference to the stone's actual weight. The term carat comes from the word *carob*, a bean that is similar to a cocoa bean in size and flavor. Centuries ago, a one-carat diamond was equal in weight to a single carob bean. A carat is standardized today at 200 milligrams. Weight can also be referred to by a point system, whereas one carat equals 100 points. (We will discuss *karats* later, in chapter 2.)

When deciding on the carat weight of your diamond, remember that bigger isn't always better. A large stone that has a low clarity rating could potentially cost less than a smaller stone that is only very slightly included. Also, because larger diamonds are more rare, the cost and value will rise exponentially as weight goes up. For example: if you have two one-carat VVS2 diamonds and one two-carat VVS2 diamond. The two-carat will be worth more than both of the one-carat stones combined.

SYNTHETIC STONES, ENHANCED DIAMONDS, AND DIAMOND SIMULANTS

The most important thing to note in this section is that enhanced stones are not the same as synthetic stones. *Enhanced diamonds* are natural but are treated with methods described next, including filling with clear substances, drilling, or changing properties with heat, pressure, or radiation to attain better color or clarity. *Synthetic stones* are created entirely in a lab and are not natural diamonds. *Diamond simulants* are not really diamonds at all but are either man-made or natural stones that closely resemble diamonds. Usually sold for a fraction of the price of a natural diamond, these stones can be great for someone who is searching for a certain look but is restrained by a budget.

Without a doubt, natural stones that are untreated are more valuable than any diamond that has been altered. Let's examine the differences among these three relatively recent innovations and what they mean in regard to your diamond purchase.

SYNTHETIC DIAMONDS

Grown entirely in a laboratory, synthetic diamonds are essentially the same in both chemical composition and crystal structure as natural diamonds. While numbers of these stones remain relatively limited, they are produced in Japan, South Africa, Russia, Ukraine, and the United States by one of two methods: HPHT (see page 35) or CVD (chemical vapor deposition) treatment.

ENHANCED DIAMONDS

Again, diamonds can be treated to achieve a better color or clarity using a variety of methods. To be legitimate, a dealer must always disclose any treatments, and it should be noted on your certificate of authenticity. Most gemological laboratories won't grade enhanced diamonds, but they will note the presence of filling on your report. These treatments inherently lower the value of your stone but may be worth it to you in order to achieve the look you want for your price point.

FRACTURE FILLING ♦ Introduced in the 1980s, this technique is based on the idea of infusing a molten glass substance into a diamond's fractures or inclusions. You might consider purchasing a *fracture-filled* diamond if you are looking for a flashy stone or fun piece at a reduced price. You might also be able to repair a cracked diamond you already own with this

A magnified view of a fracture-filled diamond.

technique. But beware, sometimes the filler can lower your stone's color grade, and excessive cleaning might damage the filler. If buying a fracture-filled diamond, shop with manufacturers who are willing to offer a lifetime guarantee.

LASER DRILLING ♦ Used to remove inclusions permanently, laser drilling relies on a tiny laser beam to tunnel into a stone. The marks left by laser drilling often look more natural than those that are fracture filled. Laser drilling does not affect the strength of a diamond.

A magnified view of a laser-drilled diamond.

HPHT TREATMENT ♦ This acronym refers to High Pressure/High Temperature treatment. This is a lab process that can change the color of some diamonds, and it is very difficult for most jewelers and gemologists to detect. Devised in the 1990s, HPHT is a threat to the industry because there is not currently a means for absolute detection.

IRRADIATION ♦ Another color treatment, irradiation merely changes the surface of the stone by producing a concentration of color where the gemstone is thinnest.

DIAMOND SIMULANTS

As an affirmed diamond lover, you probably aren't crazy about the prospect of buying a stone that could be considered a knock-off or look-alike of a natural diamond. But take note: today's diamond simulants are extremely well made and can allow you to make a fun, over-the-top purchase without breaking the bank. Here are two examples of popular diamond simulants:

CUBIC ZIRCONIA ♦ While it has a less-than-stellar connotation, cubic zirconias, or CZs, when made at their highest quality, are not visibly different from diamonds to the naked eye. They are hard enough to cut glass and can offer the customer flash at a fraction of the price of natural diamonds. If you are shopping for a high-quality CZ, look for companies that will insure their stones or that offer lifetime guarantees against breaking or chipping.

MOISSANITE ♦ A synthetic stone, Moissanite's atomic properties are different from that of a diamond but its optical properties are very similar. Priced at about one-tenth of the cost of a diamond of the same weight, Moissanite actually surpasses diamonds in the properties of fire and brilliance. If your jeweler doesn't have documentation that identifies your stone as Moissanite, you can have it independently graded by a gemological lab.

A Charles & Colvard Moissanite ring by K&G Creations set in white gold.

GRADING REPORTS AND
DIAMOND CERTIFICATION

Now that you've learned all about the properties that make up a diamond, you need to make things official. Without a doubt, it is critical to obtain a diamond certificate from a reputable gemological laboratory in order to insure and protect your purchase. A certificate will contain your diamond's characteristics, including the Four C's, and other information proving its authenticity. You will pay a fee to the lab for an impartial grading of the diamond if it is not already included in your purchase.

There are several different independent labs that you can approach to have your diamond graded. Each report will vary slightly, but all are internationally recognized (see Resources on page 128).

♦ *GIA*: The Gemological Institute of America will issue a Diamond Grading Report for your stone. Your report will contain a bevy of details as well as a diagram of internal and external characteristics and any flaws. GIA will only grade natural diamonds.

♦ *AGS*: The American Gem Society has its own Diamond Grading Laboratory that rates cut, color, and clarity on a scale of zero to 10, with zero as the most rare and desirable and 10 the least desirable. If you are looking to purchase the top grade of a round diamond, find an AGS Triple Zero. That designation denotes ideal proportions, polish, and symmetry.

♦ *EGL*: The European Gemological Laboratory has worldwide grading facilities and its certifications include specifics, such as crown height percentage and pavilion depth percentage. You can also get a condensed report known as a consultation that lists only carat weight, color grade, clarity grade, and a plotting diagram.

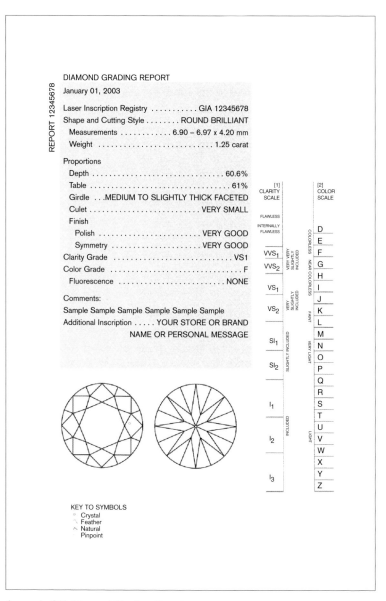

DIAMOND GRADING REPORT

January 01, 2003

REPORT 12345678

Laser Inscription Registry . . . . GIA 12345678
Shape and Cutting Style . . . . ROUND BRILLIANT
    Measurements . . . . 6.90 – 6.97 x 4.20 mm
    Weight . . . . 1.25 carat

Proportions
    Depth 60.6%
    Table 61%
    Girdle . . .MEDIUM TO SLIGHTLY THICK FACETED
    Culet . . . . VERY SMALL
Finish
    Polish . . . . VERY GOOD
    Symmetry . . . . VERY GOOD
Clarity Grade VS1
Color Grade . . . . F
    Fluorescence . . . . NONE

Comments:
Sample Sample Sample Sample Sample Sample
Additional Inscription . . . . . YOUR STORE OR BRAND
                    NAME OR PERSONAL MESSAGE

[1] CLARITY SCALE		[2] COLOR SCALE
FLAWLESS		
INTERNALLY FLAWLESS		D
		E
VVS$_1$		F
VVS$_2$		G
		H
VS$_1$		I
		J
VS$_2$		K
		L
		M
SI$_1$		N
		O
SI$_2$		P
		Q
		R
I$_1$		S
		T
		U
I$_2$		V
		W
		X
I$_3$		Y
		Z

KEY TO SYMBOLS
    ° Crystal
    ⟍ Feather
    ⌒ Natural
      Pinpoint

A sample GIA Diamond Grading Report.

- *PGS*: Relatively new, Professional Gem Services has full-service offices in both Chicago and Los Angeles that will certify your diamonds.
- *IGI*. The International Gemological Institute is one of the leading gemological facilities in the world. Besides independent jewelers, IGI provides reports to outlets including insurance companies, Internet wholesalers, and accounting and securities firms. IGI certificates are often found accompanying a purchase in retail mall jewelry stores and large chains.

CONFLICT DIAMONDS

Last, but certainly not least, your diamond purchase should initially include consideration of the serious issue of *conflict diamonds*. Now the focus of international legislation, conflict or "blood" diamonds are rough diamonds that are used by rebel movements to finance wars against legitimate governments. The trade of these stones in countries such as Angola, the Democratic Republic of Congo, and Sierra Leone has led to devastating conflict that continually threatens the lives of the people in these war-torn regions.

To combat this global crisis, the Kimberley Process was created to regulate the trade of rough diamonds. It is a voluntary system that carries strict rules of certification and origin of the diamonds shipped and sold by its participants. Today, a vast majority of rough diamonds is regulated by the Kimberley Process. Nonetheless, your retailer should know the answers to questions including:

- From what country was this diamond imported?
- In what country was this stone mined?
- Do your wholesale stone dealers and jewelry manufacturers participate in the Kimberley Process?

CHAPTER TWO

Settings and Styles for Your Personality

I NEVER WORRY ABOUT DIETS.
THE ONLY CARROTS THAT INTEREST ME ARE
THE NUMBER YOU GET IN A DIAMOND.

—*Mae West*

I T'S A FAMILIAR SCENARIO: You walk into a jewelry store that's full of alluring bits of glitter and glamour, and the fantastical world of gems causes you to forget what you were even shopping for in the first place. When the clerk inevitably asks, "What can I help you find today?" you hesitate. The trick to making a great purchase is to arm yourself with a predetermined view of the kind of woman you are and how your look and lifestyle will play into your purchase.

With your new knowledge of the shapes, sizes, and prices of your desired diamonds tucked firmly in mind, you're ready to turn those stones into an accessory. While diamonds are the perfect accoutrement for any woman's wardrobe, it is how you wear them that allows you to express your personal style.

This chapter will familiarize you with the most popular and accessible stone settings and metals that can frame your diamond. From bezel to prong and from gold to platinum, the key is to find a look that fits your lifestyle and state of mind. This chapter will also help you to uncover your "accessory personality"—the type of woman you most identify with, in relation to your sense of style. This knowledge will aid you in the quest for the perfect gem, one that will ultimately be a symbol of your unique look.

First and foremost, throw out all the rules and preconceptions you have about diamond jewelry. Today, savvy women know that diamonds do not just equal marriage. In fact, the current mindset is that diamonds are as much a symbol of independence as one of betrothal. From funky right-hand rings to slick stiletto earrings, the substance and style of diamonds can make any piece of fine jewelry dazzle.

SETTINGS AND MOUNTINGS

While you might think of settings in terms of merely how to best show off a diamond's appearance, there are other factors to consider when buying a piece of diamond jewelry. For example: How much wear and tear will the piece be getting? What is your daily routine like? How big is the stone you are setting? Considering all these factors, along with the look of each setting, will help you make an informed decision. Many traditional settings, and a few modern options, are available to enable you to find the right look for your needs.

PRONG ♦ Arguably the most traditional and universally accepted of settings, the prong, or claw, setting is loved because of its ability to show off the brilliance of a diamond to maximum effect. Here's how it works: The diamond is held in place with either four or six prongs, setting the stone above the band. Because the underside of the diamond is partially exposed, more light is able to enter and then leave the diamond, resulting in heightened brilliance. Prongs can be individualized with styles including pointed, round, flat, and v-shaped. The prong setting is especially popular in solitaire rings (rings with just one center stone and no side stones) and is prized for its ability to hold large stones securely.

CHANNEL ✦ Most often associated with wedding bands, a channel setting is great for housing smaller diamonds in pieces that will endure a lot of use. In this setting, the stones are placed directly next to one another with no metal separation. Although this setting is extremely secure, it will reduce the amount of light that enters the diamond. For pieces that are worn constantly, such as wedding or anniversary bands, the channel set allows you to carry on your day-to-day routine without worrying about your jewelry.

BEZEL ✦ In this look, a stone is completely surrounded by a rim of metal. Like the channel-set diamond, bezel-set stones are very secure while even less light is let into the stone. This setting is appreciated by women who want the least wear and tear possible to their diamonds and by those who often use their hands during the day. Be aware: the bezel setting reflects the color of the adjacent metal into your stone, so white is often the way to go when setting a diamond in this way. While the look seems contemporary, the bezel setting was often used in medieval times to set jewels into armor or weapons.

PAVÉ ✦ Related to the channel setting, stones are considered pavé set when one prong comes into contact with at least three stones. Used regularly in all jewelry, from rings and bracelets to watches, pavé diamonds add brilliance and sparkle to the overall look of a piece. This setting is best created with small round diamonds or chips.

TENSION ✦ For the ultimate in contemporary jewelry, look no further than the tension setting. In this technique, a diamond is held in place by pressure from the metal band. This setting allows the most light to penetrate the diamond, creating a truly dazzling appearance.

BAR ✦ Similar to the channel setting, the bar setting is also used in circular bands but there are no prongs to hold the stones in place. Instead, the gems are separated by thin metal bars.

 CLUSTER ✦ If you want the appearance of a larger stone, consider a cluster setting. In this configuration, a large gem is surrounded with several smaller gems. These smaller accents give the piece added sparkle and significance.

GYPSY ✦ Often used in men's pieces, the gypsy setting can also flatter the look of some women's rings. The gypsy setting uses one continuous band that comes to a thicker, dome shape at the top. The gem is set within the dome, creating a smooth, clean look. Because all but the top of the stone is surrounded by metal, there is less light reflection and, therefore, less sparkle with this setting.

FLAT-TOP ✦ Related to the gypsy setting, the flat-top's band is also broader at the top, but it is used to set faceted stones, with metal clips holding onto the gem's girdle for security. The look is modern and often perceived as less effeminate than other styles.

DIAMOND WEAR AND TEAR

While diamonds are the hardest stones on earth, they are not indestructible, and it is important to recognize that diamond jewelry is not immune to everyday hazards. For diamonds that you wear every day, make sure that you:

- Remove them during extended periods of housework or yard work. While your diamonds probably won't be scratched, they could be chipped if hit particularly hard.

- Steer clear of chlorine bleach. If you are doing household chores, don't let your precious jewelry come into contact with bleach. Chlorine will weaken your setting over time and could cause your diamond to come loose.

- If you store your jewelry while traveling or doing strenuous work, place diamonds in a fabric-lined case, separate from your other jewelry. While your diamonds will be safe among your other pieces, those pieces will not be safe among diamonds, which can and will scratch other stones and metals.

- Have your settings checked once a year. Go to a trusted jeweler and watch as they check your diamond's setting for fastness. If it's loose, have it repaired to avoid losing the stone.

METALS

First things first: when you're choosing a precious metal for your jewelry, the difference is definitely more distinct than yellow versus white. Along with considering the look of the metal, you should be informed about the properties of gold, platinum, silver, or even a more contemporary choice such as titanium. Variables such as strength, durability, and price are not difficult to compare and contrast, and making the right choices can turn a simple purchase into a family heirloom.

First, let's take a look at the two major metals used for setting diamonds: gold and platinum, and then at two less traditional choices: silver and titanium.

GOLD

Chances are good that throughout your life, you have associated gold with fine jewelry. The perception might stem from the gold herringbone bracelet you received for your first communion or bat mitzvah, or from the gold necklace you saw your father present to your mother on their anniversary. Whether white or yellow, gold has ancient roots, and its traditional overtones have made it a staple for

engagement rings, wedding bands, and other everyday pieces such as bracelets, chains, and earrings.

Here are the basics: Gold's purity is measured in *karats*. When taken from the earth, gold is naturally yellow, and that pure gold is 24 karat. As the gold is alloyed, or mixed with other metals, the purity decreases to a lower *karatage*. The other standards in the United States for gold jewelry are 18-karat, 14-karat, and 10-karat, although 22-karat is slowly catching on as an alternative. The lowest European standards are: 18-karat in France and Italy; 9-karat in England; and 8-karat in Germany. Pure gold is richer in color but softer than lower karatages.

YELLOW GOLD VS. WHITE GOLD

In today's society, many women choose to set their diamonds in white gold, because the color of the metal enhances the whiteness of the stone. When set in yellow gold, the color of the metal can reflect into the diamond and make the stone appear tinted a duller shade.

What are the advantages and disadvantages of the two colors? Proponents of yellow gold maintain that it is *real* gold, because it is the natural color of the metal when mined from the ground. Some women find that yellow gold is more flattering to their skin tones and don't want the addition of white metal to clash with the yellow-gold jewelry wardrobe they have built up over the years. Proponents of white gold point

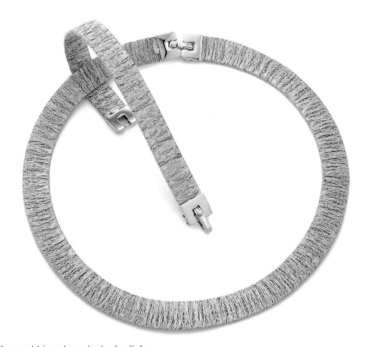

Yellow gold jewelry suite by Leslie's.

White gold bands by Artcarved.

Two-toned jewelry by Monarch Fine Jewelry.

to its ability to make a white diamond look even whiter and its compatibility with other metals, such as silver and platinum.

Compromises are available. The two-toned look has become broadly popular with fashion-forward women who want to integrate white and yellow gold into their jewelry pieces. Jewelers can also create a yellow-gold shank (the band) that contains a white-gold piece just to hold the stone. So, while the piece is primarily yellow, the metal reflected in the diamond is white.

OTHER GOLD OPTIONS

Jewelers have found even more ways to appeal to fashion-conscious consumers looking for an array of color options for their gold jewelry. Using rose, green, or even purple gold personalizes your jewelry with unique tones that can make each piece a showstopper.

Rose gold is an increasingly popular option for women who prefer wearing a warm-toned metal against their skin. Universally flattering, gold with a pinkish hue alloyed with a metal such as copper is being used more and more in upscale wristwatches and rings.

Green gold, while not widely used, is also a viable designer option. Alloyed with metals such as copper, silver, or palladium, this variant will certainly stand out from the crowd. Again, while this and other colored alloys will create excite-

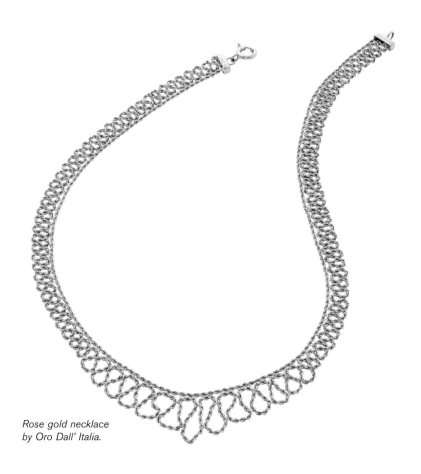

*Rose gold necklace
by Oro Dall' Italia.*

ment around a special piece of jewelry, they are not necessarily
ideal for setting a large, white diamond, as the color will reflect
into the stone.

PLATINUM

At once a staple of your grandmother's generation and a symbol of the future of fine jewelry, platinum is something of a
conundrum for today's savvy shopper. Is it retro? Is it modern? The beauty of platinum is that it can be either, and its
many desirable characteristics make it a good choice for setting diamonds into any piece of jewelry. Platinum's brilliant
natural white color makes it instantly compatible with colorless diamonds.

Platinum may seem *au courant*, but its roots are ancient and its modern heyday dates back to the early twentieth century, when Art Deco was all the rage. To set tiny stones into the geometric designs popular at the time, jewelers needed a metal that was both durable and pliable, and platinum fit the bill perfectly. Your grandmother's engagement ring or other pieces of fine jewelry may have been forged in platinum. But, at the dawn of World War II, things changed.

Los Angeles–based Tacori makes platinum vintage-inspired engagement rings.

Due to demand from the military, platinum was banned from ornamental use because its rarity prohibited too much consumption of the useful metal.

So, why has platinum's popularity skyrocketed again? First, it is extremely durable. Denser than other precious metals, it does not wear away with everyday use. Second, it is rare. Platinum is thirty-five times more rare than gold, which gives it the exclusivity that some consumers desire. Third, platinum is pure. Unlike gold, which has to be alloyed to become white, platinum is naturally white when mined. The international purity standard for platinum jewelry is 95 percent, and this purity also makes it hypoallergenic for those with sensitive skin.

Be prepared for the dent platinum will likely make in your wallet. Its rarity makes it more valuable per ounce, which will definitely translate to the price tag.

TITANIUM

Titanium, which shares many properties with platinum, is the metal of the future where jewelry is concerned. Already a standard for use in engineering, architecture, medical implants, and aerospace industries, titanium's light weight in combination with its amazing strength and durability, make it an intelligent, although relatively underappreciated, choice for fine jewelry. If you want to create a piece of jewelry that will not fade under the stress of a hectic everyday life, titanium may be just the metal for you.

Titanium and diamond hoop earrings by Boccia.

Naturally gray when mined, titanium is far more abundant than platinum but is similarly hypoallergenic. Another titanium bonus is its resistance to corrosion. If you're an ocean lover, don't fear: titanium and salt water find no fault with each other. (Gold should not be worn in chlorinated water, and silver, because it is likely to tarnish, is best kept away from salt water and chlorine). While titanium is not the average choice for setting diamonds, its uniqueness will certainly be a conversation starter, and wearing it will identify you as a progressive fashionista in the world of fine jewelry.

SILVER

Lauded for its lower price tag and accessibility, sterling silver is not the standard when it comes to setting diamonds. But, in recent years, designers have begun dotting this white metal with diamonds to offer their customers an affordable look that still lets them spoil themselves with precious stones. Sterling silver is 92.5 percent pure and is alloyed with 7.5 percent copper, which makes it more durable and strong. This is why you should look for .925 inscribed on any sterling silver jewelry that you buy. The mark confirms that your purchase is real silver.

One of silver's downfalls is that it tarnishes over time when exposed to air and moisture. However, all your silver jewelry can be easily cleaned with polish found at local drugstores and from your fine jeweler. Truthfully, silver is not your best choice for setting a diamond solitaire because of its relative informality and lower durability. Look to silver for mounting less valuable stones, colored gemstones, or fashion jewelry.

Cleaning your Diamonds in Every Setting

Diamonds, like any other surface, will get dirty, dusty, and smudged after continued wear. Cleaning methods for diamond jewelry are invariably the same, regardless of the metal surrounding the stone. You can buy cleaners that are specifically made for one metal or another, or you can use one of these three methods whenever your jewelry needs a good bath.

- **SOAP BATH** ♦ The recipe for this mix is easy: a small bowl of warm (not hot) water and any mild household liquid detergent. Jewelry can be cleaned with a soft brush until you have created lather and then rinsed with warm water. Delicately pat jewelry dry with a soft, dry cloth.

- **THE QUICK-DIP** ♦ This one is as simple as reading the directions. Buy a premade jewelry cleaner that best suits your piece of jewelry, based on all stones and metals it contains. The process usually consists of a "quick dip" in the solution followed by a rinse or by patting the piece dry.

- **ULTRASONIC CLEAN** ♦ Today, many versions of ultrasonic cleaners are available. These small machines work by creating a high-frequency turbulence in the liquid in which the jewelry is soaked. For the best results, follow precisely any directions that come with the machine.

NOTE: While these methods are safe for diamonds and precious metals, they are not safe for delicate stones such as pearls, corals, lapis, opals, amber, and, sometimes, emeralds. These pieces can be professionally cleaned, or you can dip them in plain warm water for a gentle fix for lifting dirt.

WHAT IS YOUR JEWEL TONE?
Sample Personalities to Guide Your Jewelry Search

HBO TV's MEGA HIT *Sex and the City* was beloved by women everywhere for several reasons: the fabulous fashion, the devilish men, and the backdrop of New York City, among others. But it was the four main characters who sparked a diehard obsession with most fans. Probably, you identified most strongly with one of the four women: Were you a Carrie (thoughtful, quirky, creative); a Miranda (level headed, rational, opinionated); a Charlotte (conservative, compassionate, emotional); or a Samantha (assertive, confident, unapologetic)? Although most of us embody a little of one and a little of another, you probably associate with a certain "type" when it comes to your fashion sense and lifestyle.

You may remember Carrie's trendy nameplate necklace, Charlotte's demure pearls, Miranda's no-nonsense brooches, or Samantha's can't-miss oversized earrings. Each of these looks, whether you realized it or not, helped create a character and an overall style for each woman. Don't forget that you are just as iconic and unique as each of these fictional characters were.

The five sample personalities outlined here are merely guidelines. Don't be afraid to take advice from multiple columns when it comes to choosing different components for your diamond jewelry. Take your knowledge of shapes, sizes, settings, and metals and weigh it against your own lifestyle and personal needs. Don't forget: Jewelry you choose for yourself should reflect a little something of your personality. Signature pieces have long defined the world's most stylish women from Elizabeth Taylor (the Taylor-Burton diamond) and Jackie O (Jean Schlumberger bracelets) to Coco Chanel (long, layered strands of pearls).

THE TRADITIONAL WOMAN

Far from being stodgy or boring, the traditional woman in this sense points to a classic and classy point-of-view in looks and attitude. Clues that you may be a traditionalist in terms of your jewelry: Are simple pearl or diamond studs still your standard accessory? Does your dream engagement ring come in Tiffany & Co.'s little blue box? Is Audrey Hepburn one of your style icons? Women in this category tend to dress on the conservative side in tailored clothing that stays in style from season to season.

If this sounds familiar, there are a few tips you can follow for finding a piece of diamond jewelry to fit your style. Traditional women often opt for the classic round, brilliant cut for its universally appealing shape and maximum brilliance or the princess cut for its simple and understated modernity. The Tiffany setting—in its classic four-prong—will probably be the most appealing option for a solitaire. (See chapter one, page 20 for diamond cuts, and chapter two, page 44 for settings.) If you have a two-toned wristwatch, white metal, for its simplicity and beauty, will invariably be your best choice for setting your colorless diamond.

THE CONTEMPORARY WOMAN

If the words "sleek" and "modern" define your living space or your wardrobe, you might fall into the contemporary category. Unfussy and uncluttered, your lifestyle is based on clean lines and simple good taste. Would you rather hang a piece of abstract art above your couch than a pastel Impressionist rendering? Does your wardrobe consist of solid colors in body-contouring fabrics such as silk jersey? Your jewelry box is filled with objects of a similar nature: bold pieces that seamlessly integrate stones and metal, fluid shapes that mold to the contour of the body, and geometric forms based in an artistic mindset.

Most contemporary women do not shy away from metal. Even when mounting a beautiful stone, they are not afraid to use oversized settings in rich, yellow golds or cool whites. Understated stone shapes such as dome-shaped stones (cabochons) and emerald cuts may be good choices for this woman. Other options are bezel setting; a fancy shape such as a marquise or oval for an updated, less traditional look; or tension-setting diamonds for a completely modern piece of jewelry. (See chapter one, page 20 for diamond cuts, and chapter two, page 44 for settings.)

ROBERT LEE MORRIS:
COOL AND CONTEMPORARY

An undeniable force in the world of jewelry since the 1970s, Robert Lee Morris embodies the contemporary spirit. When his pieces landed on the cover of *Vogue* in 1976, the fashion world sat up and took notice of his bold, visionary accessories. The realization of Artwear—the designers collective that he opened in Manhattan's SoHo in 1977—was to forever change the way women looked at fine jewelry. Where jewelry was once merely an extension of an outfit, now it was art.

Morris's use of metal—whether gold or sterling silver—is sleek and substantive, and the grand scale of many of his pieces has women dressing around the jewelry, rather than the other way around. "I've been known my whole career for 'bold gold jewelry,' chunky jewelry that typified the 1980s," Morris says. "The word 'gold' and Robert Lee Morris has a resonance to it in history." His collaborations with the ultimate contemporary woman's designer, Donna Karan, have been featured again and again on the runways of New York.

Recently, Morris ventured further into the world of diamonds when he joined with M. Fabrikant & Sons, the largest diamond house in America. Many of his designs are now dotted with diamonds, a move that accentuates the form and shapes of his pieces. Some of his sterling silver work can also be accented with diamonds, for a luxe look at a lower price.

Robert Lee Morris's Margarita Salt Collection marries 18-karat yellow gold and pavé-set diamonds for a look that is clean and contemporary.

THE ROCK STAR

Is your life full of flash? Do bold colors, over-the-top designs, and innate glamour characterize you? If you're not afraid to wear leather, animal prints, or a rainbow palette of makeup, you may just be a Rock Star. More clues: Your closet is full of stilettos, and plunging necklines and high hemlines may be *de rigeur*. Your jewels are similarly bold: sparkly gemstones cover dangling earrings, oversized pendants, and eye-catching cocktail rings. There is no such thing as too many accessories if you are a Rock Star; in fact, piling on the "bling" is fun and empowering.

If you're trying to match your accessories with a rock 'n' roll personality, cluster or pavé settings (see chapter two, page 44) may give you the sparkle you're looking for without having to use outrageously expensive, large stones. Platinum is the new must-have metal for today's celebrity A-listers. So, choosing the lustrous white metal may give you that extra cachet that you crave.

STEPHEN WEBSTER:
ROCK STAR JEWELER

From humble beginnings as a young gold-
smith in England, designer Stephen
Webster now counts superstars
such as Madonna, Elton John,
Ozzy Osbourne, and Christina
Aguilera as devoted fans of his
bold jewelry. If you're eager to let
your inner Rock Star shine through,
Webster's handcrafted pieces are invariably the way to go. According to

*A bracelet in 18-karat
white gold and diamonds
from Steven Webster's
Borneo collection.*

London-based Webster, the woman he designs for is "quite
confident—enough to feel very confident with her jewelry."

While his most notorious collection, Crystal Haze, is known for
its oversized, faceted colored gemstones, his recent collections
have spotlighted diamonds. Now making up 50 percent of his sales,
diamond jewelry has turned over a new leaf, in terms of the female
self-purchase. "I began the diamond focus collection because it felt
like the stigma of a woman buying her own diamonds was ending,"
Webster says. "For a while it was OK for a woman to buy colored
stone jewelry for herself because it was a fashion statement, but it
was somehow 'sad' for her to buy her own diamonds. That [mindset
is] gone now, and women are thrilled."

Because Webster's diamond designs are not based on the
solitaire, he tends to use smaller stones to create fashion-forward jewelry in collections such
as Attention Seeker, Borneo, and Tattoo. "I
probably most often use standard, brilliant-cut
round diamonds," Webster explains. "My clients
are women who want a 'look,' and the best way
to achieve that look for the right amount of
money is with smaller diamonds. You can fit a
small, round diamond into anything—any pattern,
any design." To get this glamorous, sure-to-be
noticed look, expect to spend in the

*Webster's 18-karat
white gold Pleasure
Seeker rings set
with diamonds.*

$2,500–$5,000 range for Webster's rings,
bracelets, earrings, and pendants set in 18-
karat white or yellow gold.

THE TOMBOY

If you covet comfort more than couture, it doesn't mean that you can't carry off a diamond or two. Whether you prefer sneakers to stilettos, or just appreciate menswear staples such as tweeds, argyles, and neckties in your wardrobe, there is no reason to eschew fine jewelry. Do you favor pantsuits to wrap dresses or claim fedoras and newsboy caps as daily accessories? Is your regular jewelry wardrobe honed down to a simple wristwatch or a small pendant on a chain? If you are a Tomboy, you might think that diamonds are too flashy for your lifestyle, but, rest assured, there are ways to make a statement while retaining understatement.

Women in the tomboy category can look to settings that are traditionally popular in men's jewelry, such as the flat-top or gypsy settings (see chapter two, page 40). Used with wider bands, they give a substantial look, while remaining clean and understated. If your watch is your must-wear accessory, consider a style that is embellished with a few small, round brilliants around the face. And diamond brooches or tie clips can turn any pantsuit or blazer into a study in elegance.

The Romantic

Pastels or florals may charm you, or maybe vintage details make up your most prized possessions. Even what you buy new has a touch of the Old World: a wool jacket with carved Bakelite buttons, a tablecloth trimmed in antique lace, or a chandelier strung with turn-of-the-century glass beads. If you're dressing up, you might tend toward the flowing, feminine feel of chiffons, or you might opt for princessy layers or sweet ruffles. Your jewels might have come straight from your grandmother's vault: strands of layered pearls and beads, cameos, and brooches adorn your favorite ensembles.

To accentuate your feminine style, explore Old-World diamond cuts such as the rose, Asscher, and old mine (see chapter one, page 20) for a vintage look that is back in vogue. While these cuts don't create as much brilliance as newer styles, their elegance is undeniable. To re-create authentic vintage jewelry, create your pieces from platinum. Platinum's amazing malleability allows for detailed designs, including hand carving, that will give your diamond jewelry added personality.

CHAPTER THREE

Vintage Jewelry and Red-Carpet Glamour

IT IS BETTER TO HAVE OLD SECOND-HAND
DIAMONDS THAN NONE AT ALL.

—*Mark Twain*

I N THE CONTEXT OF CLOTHING OR JEWELRY, you've heard the word "vintage" thrown around a lot lately. Perhaps you've visited a vintage shop in your area or have perused old pieces of unmarked jewelry at an antique shop. More and more women are turning to vintage fashions for numerous reasons: First, you may be able to get treasures at a bargain. Second, shoppers are able to purchase pieces that no one else will have. This allows you to create one-of-a-kind ensembles that separate you from the pack.

In both clothing and in jewelry, there are certain things to look for when shopping for vintage items. First, you have to carefully check the quality. Are there any stones loose or missing? Is the metal marked so you know it's genuine? Are any stones chipped or cracked? If you are considering buying an expensive piece of vintage diamond jewelry, it is probably best to do it at a highly regarded jewelry or antique store, and not at a vintage clothing store. The more the salesperson knows about the piece, the better. If a piece is of high value, you should also have it independently appraised to find out approximately when it was made and what it is worth (see chapter one). This appraisal is a smart idea for the initial purchase and also to insure your piece of vintage jewelry.

Vintage jewelry today is big business. Major auction houses like Christie's and Sotheby's have special auctions for vintage pieces, and normally the most expensive lots are old, "signed" (labeled from a major jewelry house) pieces that are exceptionally rare and beautiful. Women today are enamored of vintage jewelry for a few reasons. First, they appreciate the quality and beauty of jewelry from a time when everything was handmade. Second, it is a special treat to own something from another era that remains just as beautiful today. And lastly, vintage jewelry helps you to create your own look that no one else can replicate.

The first part of this chapter will give you the means to shop for vintage jewelry with confidence. Next, we will delve into two popular eras from which vintage jewelry came: Art Nouveau and Art Deco. Then you'll learn about the famous names that created many of the best vintage pieces. Finally we'll jump ahead to the 1950s and '60s; two decades with that exemplified fabulous diamond cocktail jewelry.

How to Shop for Vintage Jewelry

Let's face it: You are not a jewelry appraiser. Dates, designers, and exact techniques are best left to professionals when you are considering buying an expensive piece of jewelry.

There are a few ways, at least, to separate the real deal from a bad reproduction.

QUALITY ✦ This should be your first consideration when shopping for old pieces. Check for detailed finishes on the backs of the pieces.

ENAMEL ✦ Reproductions are often more uniform than authentic pieces. Look for variations in the shading, not for crisp, clean edges and colors.

CLASPS ✦ Vintage pieces will often have the most wear and tear on their clasps or pins. Newer jewelry will show little or no wear in these areas, which should be a signal that it was made more recently.

HALLMARKS ✦ Look for stamps or hallmarks denoting the manufacturer.

Your best bet for vintage finds is to shop at a recommended jeweler or antique shop that will guide you through the process. Again, many Deco designs were created in platinum, and for items with exceptionally high price tags, look for hallmarks that denote a jeweler, such as Tiffany & Co. or Cartier.

Art Nouveau

The Look

While a short-lived movement (from about 1890 to 1910), Art Nouveau was nevertheless an extremely important period for architecture, art, and, of course, jewelry. In the late 1800s, people started to respond to the Industrial Revolution by looking for ways to counteract the hard reality of technology and mass production. Suddenly, life forms took center stage as images of women with cascading hair and flora and fauna were incorporated into accessories. Fantasy and spirit worlds collided as flowing lines and new production techniques were established. From subject matter to materials used, Art Nouveau jewelry broke the mold and pieces from this period can be highly desirable today.

What to Look For

♦ Enameling
♦ Semi-precious stones, including moonstone, opal, freshwater pearl, or amethyst
♦ Nontraditional materials, such as shell, ivory, or bone
♦ Organic motifs, ranging from human forms to flowers to plants
♦ Curvy, free-flowing lines
♦ Hair ornaments, lockets, and necklaces

How to Wear It

More whimsical and delicate than the styles of eras to come, Art Nouveau may go best with a Romantic personality (see chapter two, page 63). Small brooches are perfect as hair accessories or on the lapel of a jacket. Art Nouveau jewelry is the perfect accessory when you are feeling ultra-feminine.

A vintage Art Nouveau enameled dragonfly brooch with diamonds studded along the tail.

Art Deco

The Look

Art Deco (c. 1910–1930) focused on geometry and symmetry. Clean-cut and streamlined, designers' style incorporated the realities of the Industrial Revolution.

So, what is the Deco look all about? Clean lines, bold colors, and careful geometry. Diamonds, in particular, enjoyed a striking renaissance. From new cuts (emerald, pear, marquise) to sparkling pavé, the white-on-white look was in. Platinum, the metal of choice for setting precious stones, enabled designers to create pieces with intricate outlines and precise shapes.

What to Look For

♦ Geometric shapes, from circles to rectangles to triangles
♦ Long necklaces (*sautoirs*), cocktail rings, linear bracelets, compacts, and cigarette cases
♦ Accent stones of sapphires, rubies, emeralds, coral, jade, or onyx
♦ Double-clip brooches (made up of two identical parts, the pieces could be worn together or separately)
♦ Crystal accents for diamonds
♦ Contrast of light and dark stones

How to Wear It

Pin brooches on your coat's lapel or in the V of the neckline of a cocktail dress or low-cut blouse. Sautoirs, the long necklaces made popular during the Deco days, are the perfect accessory for a bohemian or flapper look. Feel free to layer this kind of piece with smaller, shorter necklaces.

This sautoir, circa 1925, is a perfect example of an Art Deco necklace.

FAMOUS DECO DESIGNERS

As fashion in general became more and more important to the everyday woman, a few brand names began to take hold as staples of a fine jewelry wardrobe. These three designers rose to fame during the Art Deco period, and all three mentioned here are still at the top of their respective games.

CARTIER ♦ French jeweler Cartier began business in 1847 when Louis-François Cartier took over at the workshop of his teacher in Paris. Pierre Cartier opened its New York branch on Manhattan's famed Fifth Avenue in 1909.

Some of Cartier's most prized Art Deco pieces were made in a Chinese style, often adorned with jade and onyx. If you want to purchase an updated Chinese-style piece by Cartier, look no further than its La Baiser du Dragon (Kiss of the Dragon) collection. Pieces in this modern, twenty-first century collection include Chinese characters as well as the classic Art Deco gemstones: rubies, onyx, and diamonds.

TIFFANY & CO. ♦ Unlike Cartier, Tiffany is a uniquely American company that started out selling stationery and fancy goods in 1837. "Tiffany Blue," as the store's famous color is now known, is universally coveted by women all around the globe.

If you're looking to get the Art Deco feeling, but aren't willing to spend tens of thousands at auction, Tiffany does have modern pieces that have great Deco appeal. Diamond collections, such as the Voile and Jazz, are set in platinum, just like the original jewelry that inspired them.

BOUCHERON ♦ Frederic Boucheron, the company's founder, started his namesake company in 1858 in Paris and built it to become a pioneer among jewelers.

Stunning cigarette cases ornately detailed with onyx, enamels, and gold to tassel jewelry dotted with platinum and seed pearls—Boucheron has quite a legacy when it comes to Deco designs. Within today's offerings, you can look to the L'eau à la Bouche collection or Boucheron's most geometric modern designs.

1930s-1940s: Late Art Deco to Retro

The Look

Glamorous diamond jewelry was still very much in vogue in the late 1930s (Late Art Deco) and 1940s ("Cocktail" or "Retro"). Instead of thin, detailed platinum settings, other metals, especially gold, took center stage in the shape of three-dimensional waves, curls, and curves. Bows and knots were highly fashionable and are seen over and over again on clips, brooches, and necklaces. Pieces that were actually static were set apart by a sense of cascading, wavy motion.

Platinum, banned from ornamental use in wartime, sat on the sidelines as gold—especially in pinks and yellows—became the fashion. Designers often stamped out thin sheets of gold that could be rendered to look heavier than it actually was.

What to Look For

- Motifs including bows, knots, feathers, and flowers
- Three-dimensional aspects that evoke movement, such as waves or curls
- Bulky, oversized pieces
- Gold mesh
- Cocktail rings

An emphasis on shape, metal, and implied motion characterize jewelry, such as this feather-shaped brooch from the cocktail era of jewelry.

How to Wear It

Your best bet may be searching your grandmother's jewelry box for finds that you can wear now. You will probably want to pass on wearing a lot of the figurine or animals popular at the time, but definitely dig out anything in a bow or flower shape. Designers such as Vera Wang, whose high-end jewelry line is a favorite among celebrities, used the bow as a centerpiece of one of her recent collections—a nod to 1940s glamour, perhaps?

1950s-1960s

THE LOOK

Extravagance—and diamonds—were in. In fact, one of today's most recognizable slogans, "A Diamond is Forever," was made popular in the 1950s by the De Beers Diamond Corporation, and 1953 was the year that Marilyn Monroe sang "Diamonds Are a Girl's Best Friend." In the 1950s, flowers and bows remained a major motif and animal designs were everywhere. The 1960s look was more abstract, as symmetry became nearly outdated. Diamonds were often set alongside semiprecious stones such as coral and turquoise, or were channel set.

WHAT TO LOOK FOR

- ◆ Short, gem-laden necklaces and brooches
- ◆ Animal motif brooches
- ◆ Marquise-, pear-, and brilliant-cut diamonds juxtaposed against one other
- ◆ Asymmetrical designs, curved edges

Woven gold combines with diamonds for a mod 1960s look.

HOW TO WEAR IT

The necklace is a major accessory of the fashion elite, and versions from the '50s and '60s are often bold, chunky and unusual. Pair a singular piece with the ubiquitous black cocktail dress or a simple white shirt. Match vintage fabric prints, such as those from famed designers Pucci or Missoni, with diamonds accented with colored stones of various sizes and cuts for a truly unique, unconventional look.

Jewelry that incorporated curves and implied motion, such as this diamond-encrusted brooch, were popular in the 1950s.

Red-Carpet Glamour:
How the Stars Do It

The world of celebrity is a constant influence on our style, whether we admit to it or not. Big-name designers dress the stars for free because they understand that the masses will want to emulate the look. Moreover, today's obsession with celebrity lifestyle (gossip magazines such as *US Weekly* and *People* are more popular than ever) gives us insight into every label in an A-lister's closet.

So how much should we copy and how much of our look should be unique? The most important thing to note, with jewelry, is that accessories will have a dramatic impact on your entire ensemble. Whether you like to keep it simple or pile it on, jewels can inevitably turn the most modest A-line dress into a work of art. In this section, we will take a look at four famous celebrity ensembles and why they work for that particular star. From the earrings to necklaces and beyond, these famous women are known for their ability to accentuate their personalities in ways that are both interesting and appropriate.

JACQUELINE KENNEDY

Style icon Jackie Kennedy knew how to keep it simple. While she may be better known for her oversized black sunglasses, Jackie's jewelry choices in the 1960s were perfectly suited to her public persona as American royalty.

In this image, Jackie keeps her accessories to a minimum: a three-strand pearl necklace, dainty pearl and diamond earrings, and a small diamond brooch. Each element radiates class and distinction and is just a little more than the average woman might dare to pull off.

DAY VS. NIGHT JEWELRY ♦ By choosing a three-strand rather than a single strand, Jackie dressed up the outfit and made a statement suitable for a style icon. Style note: Don't wear daytime jewels with eveningwear. If you wear a simple diamond pendant for day, a more extravagant diamond necklace will be in order for a special occasion. Many women wrongly pair their everyday accessories with cocktail dresses or even ball gowns, and more often than not, the proportions are wrong and the jewels don't match the dress or the occasion.

SPLASHES OF SPARKLE ♦ The brooch, which Jackie placed flawlessly, let people know that she had personal style without going over the top. By adding a dash of diamonds to an all-white outfit, she ensured that extra sparkle. Take that same idea to heart: When you are dressing up, the best way to attract attention is with a little added shimmer.

Elizabeth Taylor

There is no one who can wear and appreciate jewelry quite like the *grande dame* Elizabeth Taylor. And, there was no piece of jewelry quite like the 69-carat Taylor-Burton Diamond, so named after it was bought by Elizabeth's then-husband Richard Burton, for an exorbitant fee, directly from Cartier.

Elizabeth knew the Taylor-Burton did not need any distraction, and she wisely created an outfit that would do the stone justice when planning for the 1970 Academy Awards. Her lilac dress, created by famed costume designer Edith Head, not only offset Elizabeth's famous violet eyes but also perfectly framed—and did not distract from—her jewelry.

NECKLINES ♦ Elizabeth chose a plunging neckline with the enormous Taylor-Burton Diamond. The v-shape of the chain was mimicked in the dress, creating a flattering line for the eye to follow. If you have a high neckline, skip the necklace, and go for earrings. Décolletage, on the other hand, is ideal for a drop necklace, and will perfectly show off an important piece of jewelry.

DON'T OVER-ACCESSORIZE ♦ Take a hint from Liz: if you have one dominant piece of jewelry, offset it with smaller pieces that will enhance, rather than detract from, the effect. Taylor chose small diamond drops, and little else, to complete a look that was extravagant but not gaudy.

MADONNA

With Madonna, an omnipresent fashion chameleon, one always expects the unexpected. Her arrival at the 1991 Academy Awards on the arm of the King of Pop, Michael Jackson, was already awash in hoopla. Channeling Marilyn Monroe, Madonna chose a long, beaded white gown and a bevy of Harry Winston diamond jewelry. While not over-accessorizing is a tip in this section, Madonna's entire outfit was geared toward excess. Her goal was to capture the spotlight and to keep it. In this, she was certainly a success.

THEMES CAN WORK ♦ If you are dressing for an elaborate occasion—a theme party or a lavish black tie—it may be your chance to pile on the jewels. Madonna kept her pieces in the same family by wearing all white diamonds for an overall shimmery effect. If you want to pull off this look, try to stick to jewelry from the same era or that has a similar style and feel.

BE EXTRAVAGANT NOW AND THEN ♦ Every once in a while it's fun to be over the top. Jewelry can make you feel adventurous, flirtatious, and just plain beautiful. Don't always save your favorite pieces for special occasions. Jewelry is meant to be worn and appreciated, not kept in a vault.

NICOLE KIDMAN

Known nearly as much for her stellar fashion sense as she is for her gifted acting abilities, Nicole Kidman realizes that accessories and clothing are sometimes one and the same. At the 2003 Cannes Film Festival, where Nicole was promoting her film *Dogville*, she donned an exquisite floral-print dress by Italian designer Pucci that was decorated at the collar with magnificent multicolored gems and diamonds from Italian designer Bulgari. Matching Bulgari cuffs (not shown here) completed the look.

COLOR ♦ This look proves that color on color can be a good thing. With her gown a swirl of bright shades, the multicolored cuffs from Bulgari's Allegra collection, serve to bring out the eye-catching colors. The point here is not to get too matchy-matchy. Kidman knows that the exact colors don't have to match; they merely have to accentuate the palette she is wearing. You should realize that you don't have to wear pink diamonds with a pink dress, but, in fact, colored diamond accents will add something to your ensemble.

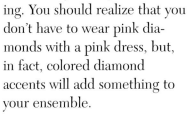

CHAPTER FOUR

Shop Till You Drop: Tips for Diamond Hunting

MONEY CANNOT BUY HEALTH, BUT I'D SETTLE
FOR A DIAMOND-STUDDED WHEELCHAIR.

—*Dorothy Parker*

Y OU'VE DONE YOUR HOMEWORK and now it's finally time to get down to the part of this book that is all business: shopping. A necessity for some women but a professional sport for others, the art of shopping should not be overlooked. There is nothing like the exhilaration of finding a good sale, or making a purchase that will be used for years to come. But, alas, most good shoppers know that while instinct plays a factor, practice does make perfect. The more you are in stores comparing products, the better you will be at weeding out the trash among the treasures.

This chapter will put you on the path to jewelry store know-how. From small mom-and-pop stores to the überchains to the Internet and television wholesalers, there are things to embrace and beware of in each shopping situation. Besides helping you to pick the right jeweler, this chapter will also give you practical advice on the right questions to ask, the best way to comparison shop, and how to appear like a seasoned pro when it comes to stones and metals.

Once you are a veritable encyclopedia of shopping information, we'll stop for a moment to consider the diamond that you've been eyeing. Because you are now the expert, this chapter will give you ways to choose and display subtly, but knowingly, the right stone for your personality and lifestyle.

So put on your comfortable shoes, grab a bottle of water and a large tote bag, and let's get ready to shop!

The Basics of Shopping

For many women, shopping for jewelry—especially fine jewelry—is not second nature. Girls have been brought up to assume that jewels will be bought for them as gifts—from gold chains for first communions and bat mitzvahs to engagement rings down the road. While you've probably bought many smaller items or accessories in your life, bigger purchases are often saved for milestone gifts such as birthdays or anniversaries. But, now that you've graduated from the silver kiosks at your local strip mall to bigger and better things, the time has come to make sure you have your wits about you at the counter.

Finding a Reliable Jeweler

Just as you trust your teeth to a particular dentist or your car to a certain mechanic, you wouldn't want to buy your fine jewelry and diamonds from just any jeweler. Recognizable chain stores are always a good indicator of reliability, but don't overlook your local, small retailers for knowledge and personal attention. So, regardless of whether you choose to buy your diamonds at a large discount store or from the local jeweler, there are a few major things to look for and consider when making a major purchase.

Comparison Shopping

As with any purchase, the best shoppers take the time to look around and weigh their options before buying things that they need or even just want. From groceries to automobiles, most women want to make sure they are getting the best deal and the most for their money. There is no better way to feel confident about a purchase than to comparison shop at different stores and via different channels in order to get not only the best deal, but also your dream jewels.

There is nothing wrong with exploring all your options when buying a diamond. Buying jewelry at a major discount

Checklist for Comparison Diamond Shopping

	Jeweler #1	Jeweler #2	Jeweler #3
Name of Store	_____	_____	_____
Credentials and Equipment (check if store has)	☐ Graduate Gemologist	☐ Graduate Gemologist	☐ Graduate Gemologist
	☐ Gem Lab	☐ Gem Lab	☐ Gem Lab
	☐ Master Set (for Diamond)	☐ Master Set (for Diamond)	☐ Master Set (for Diamond)
	☐ Certified Insurance Appraiser	☐ Certified Insurance Appraiser	☐ Certified Insurance Appraiser
♦ Carat Weight	_____	_____	_____
♦ Color (D–Z or t/s/h)*	_____	_____	_____
♦ Clarity (flawless–1)	_____	_____	_____
♦ Cut Proportions	_____	_____	_____
Table %	_____	_____	_____
Crown Angle	_____	_____	_____
Girdle	_____	_____	_____
Pavilion %	_____	_____	_____
Culet Size	_____	_____	_____
♦ Symmetry	_____	_____	_____
♦ Mounting Information	_____	_____	_____
♦ Metal	_____	_____	_____
♦ Workmanship	_____	_____	_____
♦ Manufacturer	_____	_____	_____
♦ Weight	_____	_____	_____
♦ Price	_____	_____	_____
♦ Comments	_____	_____	_____
	_____	_____	_____
	_____	_____	_____

* D–Z are color grades for diamonds. Tone, saturation, and hue (t/s/h) describe colored stones. For example, a sapphire might be described as:
t=medium dark
s=strong
h=violetish blue

Using a comparison shopping list can help you narrow the choices to the best diamond for your dollar.

store or on a home shopping channel does not mean that it is automatically of a lesser quality, and in today's society, the stigma of shopping at nontraditional venues has virtually disappeared. The most important things to consider are, first, that you are getting the diamond of your dreams, and second, that the place you are shopping is accredited and willing to assure that your diamond is what they are advertising.

No matter what channel you use, use a checklist for comparison shopping. By putting your wants, needs, and all the relevant information down on paper, you will be able to see the pros and cons of each venue's diamond side by side. This checklist should include store credentials, all the relevant diamond information regarding cut, carat weight, clarity, color, and other factors such as settings and pricing. In addition, always inquire about a store's return policy before you buy something. Some stores will offer a full refund while others offer only a store exchange.

INDEPENDENT RETAILERS

Sometimes known as mom-and-pop stores, independent retailers are those stores not tied to national chains, although there may be more than one location or branch. Many of these stores are family owned, but that certainly doesn't mean that they are not well established or equally as reputable as larger national chains. Often times, independent retailers have been fixtures in their communities for years, meaning exemplary customer service and added value for a consumer. Why added value? You can count on these local jewelers to be around for repairs, returns, and future purchases.

So how can you distinguish one local jeweler from another? Word-of-mouth is usually the best and most reliable factor. Ask around in your community to see where friends have made successful purchases, and where they have received the best personal attention. Another great way to assure that a local jeweler is reputable is to ask if they have industry organization memberships.

Luckily, the jewelry industry has many valuable resources in place to help you with your search for the perfect jeweler. Besides your local Better Business Bureau (BBB) or Watchdog UK, you can look for stores that are accredited by organizations like the Jewelers of America (JA) or stores that are registered members of the Gemological Institute of America (GIA), American Gemological Society (AGS), International Gemological Institute (IGI), or the European Gemological Laboratory (EGL-USA).

If you are shopping in North America, Jewelers of America may be one of your best resources for jewelry-specific shopping questions. The national association for retail jewelers, JA has more than 11,000 members nationwide, and its mission is to provide customers with information and education about fine jewelry. Finding your local JA jeweler is as simple as heading to the website

JEWELERS OF AMERICA

The Jewelers of America logo.

(www.jewelers.org) and using the JA jeweler database, searchable by city and state. In addition, all JA members are easily spotted by the blue J logo in their windows noting the current year.

So what does it mean to be a member of JA? Member jewelers sign an annual ethics statement, and they have access to all the most current educational programs that the industry has to offer. These jewelers are proud to hold themselves to industry standards. But note: Just because a jeweler is not a JA member does not mean that they are not trustworthy. JA is just another way to verify that the jeweler you choose will be reliable and educated.

Another great industry resource in North America is the Jewelers Vigilance Committee (JVC). This not-for-profit trade organization was put into place to maintain the jewelry industry's standards. Since its inception in 1912, the JVC has been acting as a distinguished resource for both retailers and consumers. Shoppers can use the JVC as a resource bank for

JVC logo.

any jewelry question—general or specific—and also as a legal mediator should any problems arise with a purchase.

You can ask to see if a jeweler is a member of JVC, or log on to the website (www.jvclegal.org) to get more information on finding local member stores. The JVC can also help you find a jewelry appraisal expert or answer any legal questions you may have regarding sales or ethics. Look for the JVC logo when you are shopping, for extra insurance that you are dealing with a reputable store.

All accrediting organizations hold their members to high industry standards internationally. Please refer to the Resources section, beginning on page 128, for an extensive listing of international diamond industry contacts.

NATIONAL JEWELRY CHAIN STORES

If you are traditionally a mall shopper, a national chain store setting may seem the most comfortable and familiar to you. These well-known stores are most often found in mall settings and can be every bit as accommodating and service-oriented as local independents. Because of their buying power, these stores can often offer good prices and big sales that will entice customers.

BRANDED DIAMONDS

Another factor to consider at many big chains is the choice of branded diamonds. These are diamond cuts developed by the particular store and sold under a trademarked name. While these cuts may be extremely similar to other cuts on the market, they have a distinguishing characteristic that allows the store to market it as its own. Some stores create major market-

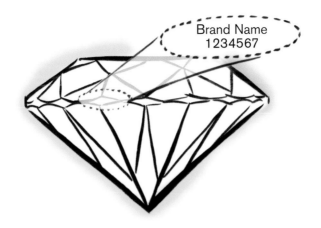

An illustration of a branded diamond inscription.

ing campaigns around their diamonds or run special promotions surrounding them. The bottom line is that a diamond's fancy name shouldn't be the main factor in making a purchase. A knowledgeable sales person, a reputable grading certificate, and a fair price should top your list when buying a diamond.

There are, however, a few reasons that a branded diamond could be a smart choice. First of all, if a diamond is branded, it means that the store stands behind its product and is ensuring that it is a quality stone. Second, it may appeal to your personal sense of cachet and desirability.

A way that many jewelers mark their branded diamonds is with a microscopic inscription on the stone that can be seen under a loupe (a jeweler's magnifying glass). The registration number of the stone, also on the certificate of authenticity, is laser inscribed onto the diamond itself. This code distinguishes your stone from any other and may give you a sense of security, a third reason to purchase a branded diamond.

You should be aware that there is usually a price markup for branded diamonds. Just as when you buy an authentic handbag from Louis Vuitton or a scarf from Burberry, you are paying for the privilege of owning that particular brand name.

TOP FIVE NORTH AMERICAN RETAIL JEWELRY CHAINS

(National Jeweler Magazine, 2004)

	Zale Corp.	Sterling Jewelers	Friedman's	Fred Meyer Jewelers	Whitehall Jewelers
# of Stores	2,230	1,103	709	445	384
Locations	50 states, Puerto Rico, Canada	45 states	20 states	38 states	38 states
Store names	Bailey Banks & Biddle, Gordon's Jewelers, Mappins Jewellers, Peoples Jewellers, Piercing Pagoda, Zales Jewelers, Zales Outlet	Belden Jewelers, Friedlander's Jewelers, Goodman Jewelers, Jared the Galleria of Jewelry, J.B. Robinson Jewelers, Kay Jewelers, LeRoy's Jewelers, Marks & Morgan Jewelers, Osterman Jewelers, Roger's Jewelers, Shaw's Jewelers, Weisfield Jewelers	Friedman's Jewelers	Barclay Jewelers, Fox's Jewelers, Fred Meyer Jewelers, Littman Jewelers	Lundstrom Jewelers, Marks Bros. Jewelers, Whitehall Co. Jewelers
Website	www.zalecorp.com	www.signetgroupplc.com	www.friedmans.com	www.fredmeyerjewelers.com	www.whitehalljewelers.com

TOP UK JEWELRY RETAILERS

Credit: Signet Group plc., National Association of Goldsmiths

Name	# of Stores	Annual Sales (£m)
H Samuel	407	286
Ernest Jones	197	209
Goldsmiths	170	149
Warren James	120	80
Beaverbrooks	55	65
F Hinds	107	60
Half Price Jewelers	57	48
Fraser Hart	30	n/a
Linkks of London	20	n/a
Mappin & Webb	17	n/a

EUROPE: T-COMMERCE REVENUES 2004

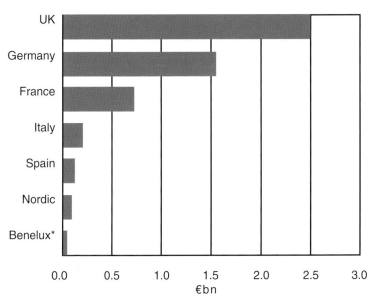

*Belgium, The Netherlands, Luxembourg

If you want to do your homework regarding the biggest retail jewelry chains, you can research the top five largest with relative ease. One thing to be aware of is that corporations own stores under various brand names. For example, whether you're shopping at a Bailey Banks & Biddle or a Gordon's Jewelers, they are both under the Zale Corp. umbrella. The same will be true for international chain stores.

SALES AND PROMOTIONS

There's no doubt that you will find sales in nearly any venue that sells jewelry, but discounting is widely seen at large chain strores. Oftentimes they can afford to discount because they are buying in bulk, allowing them to purchase at a lower price. While there is never anything wrong with a great sale, there are a couple of things to beware of when trying to get a good deal. Keep these tips in mind when shopping for jewelry through *any* venue, not just at chain stores.

- ◆ *Exaggerated discounts.* When you see promotions for values of 50 percent, 60 percent, or even 70 percent off, there are a few questions you can ask that will validate what the merchant is promising. Inquire as to whether the jewelry was ever sold at the regular price and for how long. By finding out the reference or retail price, you can shop around and see if they exaggerated that value in order to make the sale seem more enticing.
- ◆ *Trademarks.* Look closely at jewelry for markings that distinguish the piece as authentic. Look for the karat mark on gold (14K, 18K) and the Pt symbol on platinum. Anything less than 10K cannot be sold as "real" gold in the United States. The lowest European gold standards are: 18-karats in France and Italy; 9-karats in England; and 8-karats in Germany.

♦ *Mail order*. Contact your local Better Business Bureau or Watchdog UK before sending money to any post office box or unknown company. With no brick-and-mortar location to go to if something goes wrong, you want to make sure that you have a reliable contact before you make any payments.

TELEVISION SHOPPING CHANNELS

Television shopping is a growing presence in the jewelry sector. For example, in North America, the Home Shopping Network (HSN) recorded 70 million customers in 2001 with 27 percent of business owed to the jewelry category. Similarly, QVC (Quality, Value, Convenience) reached 141 million households worldwide in 2002, and 31 percent of its broadcasting was jewelry. In 2004, Jewelry Television teamed with Comcast to provide another 3.2 million U.S. customers with shopping opportunities via digital cable.

Outside of North America, television commerce continues to grow. The major players in the "T-commerce" market are the UK and Germany. The UK has six home shopping channels, while Germany's power station is HSE-Germany, based outside of Munich. (See chart, page 95.) Be aware: Jewelry shopping via television outside of North America features a large variety of costume jewelry and a small amount of high-end diamond pieces. This can be a great venue for purchasing inexpensive diamond pavé pieces that offer genuine sparkle without a high price tag.

What are some of the reasons that people turn to TV to shop? First and foremost, it's convenient. With the push of a few buttons you can have something delivered direct to your home with no hassle, lines, or travel time. You can also easily have gifts delivered to loved ones or friends. Shoppers also appreciate the discounted prices available on TV shopping channels. Seeing a price tag slashed in half is always good incentive for a purchase. Here are some tips to keep in mind when shopping from home via television:

TOP FOUR U.S. TV SHOPPING NETWORKS

(National Jeweler Magazine, 2004)

	QVC	HSN	ShopNBC	Jewelry TV by ACN
Viewership	85 million U.S. households	81 million U.S. households	53 million U.S. households	65 million U.S. households
Estimated Jewelry and Watch Sales in 2003	$1.2 billion	$425 million	$400 million	$250 million
Jewelry/Watch Sales percentage of total	25%–30%	25%	65%	N/A
Website	www.qvc.com	www.hsn.com	www.shopnbc.com	www.acntv.com
Additional info	A recent push has been made toward higher-end merchandise like diamonds, 18-karat gold, and platinum. Online sales count for an estimated 11% of total revenues.	Jewelry has been scaled back in favor of health, beauty, and home lines. Jewelry focuses on branded lines, celebrity lines, and designer collections.	Formerly known as Value Vision. Jewelry is ShopNBC's top-selling category. Internet sales represent 18% of total sales.	Formerly known as America's Collectibles Network. Jewelry TV's mix is about 70% jewelry and 30% gemstones.

TOP FIVE INTERNATIONAL T.V. SHOPPING NETWORKS

Country	Australia	Brazil	Germany	Japan	UK
Network	TVSN	Shoptime	HSE Germany	SHOP Channel	QVC UK
Website	www.itvsn.com.au	www.shoptime.com.br	www.hse24.de	www.shopch.jp	www.qvcuk.com
Year Launched	1996	1995	1995	1997	1993
Products offered	Expect 9-karat gold and small, relatively inexpensive diamond items.	Diamonds are not the focus on this shopping channel—metals mainly prevail. Pendants and bracelets in sterling silver and 18-karat gold are big sellers.	London Collection, a selection of costume fashion jewelry, is one of the station's biggest hits. Also available in Switzerland and Austria.	Targets women interested in improving the quality of their lifestyles with unique products; jewelry is not the focus.	Smaller diamond cluster items prevail in 9-karat gold. Diamond rings range between £50–150.

- *Be a savvy spender.* When you are making a significant purchase, it is always better to see the jewelry in person and deal with a salesperson one-on-one so you can vouch for the piece's quality and value. Large diamond purchases are better left to educated professionals who can guide you through each step.
- *Check details online.* All the shopping networks have websites that can be searched to find the product you want to buy. Look specifically for karat weight of gold and setting information. Very importantly, you want to find out if stones have been treated or enhanced in any way. If this information is not available online, call the network directly to get details.
- *Look for warranty information.* Again, the manufacturer's warranty information should be available online for every product you want to buy. If not, you can call the network directly and speak to a customer representative to find out all relevant information.
- *Look for branded items.* Just like branded diamonds, well-known designers who put their name on their product are standing behind their work. Many big-name designers have created lower-priced lines specifically for

television shopping channels. If you find a brand that you have purchased via TV that you like, it may be a great reason to stick with it.

♦ *Know your measurements.* To minimize returns, have your ring size and preferred chain size for necklaces and bracelets on hand when making a purchase.

INTERNET SHOPPING

The idea of shopping online comprises many different things. You may be logging on to buy a piece from your favorite retailer that you've already seen in person. You might be buying from an artisan who doesn't have a store you can go to. Or, you might be browsing eBay for a good price on a stone. Whatever your preference, there are many different things to consider when making a jewelry purchase over the Web.

SHOPPING SAFELY ONLINE

Who doesn't love shopping from the convenience of their home? You can browse in your pajamas, never have to look for a parking spot, and avoid piped in Muzak altogether. Whether it's 3 a.m. or during your lunch break, the Web is always open for business. The bottom line as far as the Internet is concerned: You don't have to fear online shopping. If you pay attention to the details, you should be safe and completely satisfied with your experience. Note: For major purchases, online may not be the best way to shop. Jewelry is always ideally tried on and examined before any purchase.

Shop Till You Drop: Tips for Diamond Hunting

- *Shop with respected companies.* The anonymity of the Internet allows anyone to set up shop and look like a reputable store. If you don't know a merchant, you can ask for a paper catalog to be mailed to your home. Also always know the return and refund policy ahead of time.
- *Pay by credit card.* In addition to having an indisputable receipt for a purchase, buying with a credit card will protect you by government legislation, giving you the right to dispute charges and temporarily withhold payment if a merchant is under investigation. In addition, some credit card companies offer additional insurance if something goes wrong.
- *Keep records.* Print out and keep any confirmations or receipts for jewelry you buy online.
- *Use a secure browser.* This tip refers to the navigation software you use to search the Web. Secure browsers scramble purchase information such as your credit card number and personal information, to keep buying safe.
- *File complaints.* If something goes wrong with an online transaction, and you are shopping in the United States, don't hesitate to contact the Federal Trade Commission (FTC) to report fraudulent practices. You can file complaints online or visit www.ftc.gov for contact information.

In the UK, an organization called TrustUK is the group to contact when you want to buy online safely. TrustUK is a non-profit organization endorsed by the government that was created specifically to help consumers buy online with confidence. When you see the TrustUK hallmark on a company's website, you will know that they adhere to well-established policies on ethics and standards, including privacy, secure payments, and customer service.

In addition, a group called Consumer Direct helps and advises consumers in the UK. Besides making complaints about a company or service, the website or operators will advise you on your rights as a consumer, supply you with fact sheets and provide you with information on counterfeit goods, scams, and unsafe products.

NAVIGATING EBAY AND AUCTION SITES

Since its inception in 1995, the eBay auction website has become the most popular shopping destination on the Internet with more than 100 million registered shoppers. Jewelry items are a major eBay draw. On any given day, nearly 50,000 items are listed under the jewelry/watches category. Auction sites can be a great way to find a hard-to-get item or just to browse for unexpected treasures. As eBay is an international company, the same rules and guidelines apply worldwide. Here are a few tips for shopping on eBay:

♦ *Look at the seller "feedback".* This term refers to a seller's online reputation with other buyers. Every seller's score is posted with his or her sale information. This is eBay's version of word-of-mouth.

♦ *Understand buyer protection.* eBay's main form of payment is PayPal, a secure system with a global network allowing customers to buy and sell in more than forty-five countries, and in currencies such as U.S., Canadian, and Australian dollars, euros, yens, and pounds sterling.

♦ *Demand authenticity.* If you are purchasing a diamond online, make sure that the seller is enclosing an authentic grading report from a lab such as GIA, IGI, EGL, or AGS (see page 37).

♦ *Don't just buy for price.* Even if what you are seeing on eBay is a great price, do some comparison shopping first. Look at what the value would be for the same stone or piece in a regular retail setting. If you are someone who likes to try on jewelry before you make a purchase, eBay may not be the right venue for you.

TOP FIVE NORTH AMERICAN DISCOUNT STORES

(National Jeweler Magazine, 2004)

	Wal-Mart	Target	Costco	Kmart	Kohl's
Estimated U.S. Retail Jewelry/Watch Sales in 2003	$2.5 billion	$450 million	$375 million	$200 million	$160 million
Jewelry/Watch Sales Percentages of Total Sales	1%	1%	1%	1%	1%–2%
Other Store Names	N/A	Mervyn's, Marshall Field's	N/A	N/A	N/A
Website	www.walmart.com	www.target.com	www.costco.com	www.kmart.com	www.kohls.com
Certification	IGI (International Gemological Institute)	IGI	Costco-generated GG appraisal with all diamonds, IGI certification with 1 carat diamonds, GIA certification with 1.25 carat diamond or larger	RGI (Royal Gemological Institute)	IGI
Miscellaneous	In 2002 started selling Keepsake brand diamond jewelry.	Continues to focus on position as upscale discounter.	Has upgraded diamond assortment and is carrying higher price points.	After bankruptcy is focused on controlling costs.	Focus is on name brands at discount prices.

DISCOUNT STORES AND SUPERCENTERS

You may be one of those women who just aren't comfortable shopping for her diamonds an aisle over from her produce. But, if you aren't one to get hung up on conventional jewelry shopping, you may find great deals on both name brands and generic pieces at supercenters or warehouse clubs.

The rules of discount shopping are the same as at any other retailer: Ask questions, demand certification, and comparison shop. All top discount retailers provide certification for their diamonds, and each has its own return or exchange policies.

THE GIRL'S GUIDE TO GETTING THE DIAMOND YOU WANT

Tips and Techniques for the Savvy Woman

OK, so now you know how to shop for the diamonds you want (and deserve). But, every so often, there is a piece of diamond jewelry that you'd rather acquire by alternate means—for example, as a gift from someone you love. Whether it's the long-desired engagement ring or a token to symbolize an anniversary or birthday, don't let your newly acquired knowledge be overlooked by your friends, family, and loved ones.

Just as no one likes a pushy hinter, loved ones are also happier to buy a gift that they know the receiver will like. There are only a few swift moves that separate you from the diamond of your dreams. Here, outlined in simple tips, are the best ways to pass on your diamond education to a potential gifter while still staying under the radar.

◆ *Tip #1: Have information mailed.* While it might seem a little obvious to leave brochures from grading laboratories lying around the house, you can go online and request that information be sent via mail. To make this authentically random, request that the information be sent to both yourself and the potential gifter. Then, when it is received, it will seem more like a mass mailing than a hint.

♦ *Tip #2: Educate friends.* Unlike the occasions when they need directions, guys are eager to ask for help when they are shopping for diamonds. The first person they will probably go to is your best friend, so make sure that she is up on her 4 C's and your favorite setting. The more she knows, the closer your significant other will get to your perfect jewel.

♦ *Tip #3: Have a favorite jeweler.* If you are consistently buying your own jewelry from a certain store, your potential gifter will probably hit the same location to buy an important jewelry gift for you. Let your usual salesperson know what styles and sizes you are interested in so that he or she can tip off your significant other when he comes in to shop.

♦ *Tip #4: Let a friend take the fall*. If you have a friend whose ring (or bracelet or necklace) style is close to what you are looking for, ask them to be assertive for you. Next time you are all together, get her to show off the piece of jewelry by claiming it was newly cleaned or refinished. It will be the perfect time to offhandedly remark that it is just the style that you would have chosen for yourself.

CHAPTER FIVE

Female Empowerment and Diamonds

I NEVER HATED A MAN ENOUGH TO
GIVE HIM DIAMONDS BACK.
—*Zsa Zsa Gabor*

YOU FINALLY HAVE ALL the information you need to make an informed diamond purchase. The Four C's; check. Insurance and grading; check. Settings and styles; check. Where to shop; check. The final thing to learn and remember is that there's no point to wearing diamonds unless they make you feel beautiful, fabulous, and empowered. Forget the old notion that diamonds have to signify someone else's love for you. In the twenty-first century, a diamond can express the love you have for yourself.

This chapter will trace the origins of diamond fashion and why today's women have completely rewritten the rules about diamond jewelry. We'll also take a closer look at some of the more holistic and spiritual qualities that diamonds supposedly possess. Next, we'll examine the recent Right-Hand Ring campaign implemented by De Beers and find out why it's a good thing for both diamonds and independent women.

Finally, we'll address the concept of "bling"—wearing loud, in-your-face diamond jewelry as a status symbol. A new trend sported by both men and women, bling may have started out with the rich and famous, but its ideals and origins definitely say something about modern society. Who are the world's most famous women who are consistently dripping in diamonds, and how have their tastes rubbed off on the public at large?

They say, "If you've got it, flaunt it." Now that you know how to get it, it's time to let those diamonds shine!

Diamonds as Ancient History

First let's get a little scientific. The story of diamonds begins not with a ring or a necklace, but with space and time. About 3.3 billion years ago, a little more than a billion years after our solar system was formed, diamonds got their start when they were born from pressure on carbon deposits up to 120 miles (200 km) below the Earth's surface. Diamonds take so long to form that every one is at least 990 million years old. That price tag makes a little more sense now, right?

Moving ahead a few billion years, the origin of modern diamonds began in India more than 1,000 years ago. It was here that diamonds were first mined and coveted for their hardness and brilliance. In Sanskrit, diamonds were most commonly known as *vajra*, or "thunderbolt." Diamonds were already known to be valuable as early as the fourth century BCE. Even then, diamonds were distributed differently among different castes of the population because of their intrinsic value and appeal.

This separation of the rich and poor held true through the years until diamonds were seen on royalty in Europe around the thirteenth century. Not the centerpieces of accessories, these small diamonds were merely accents for other, more available gems, such as pearls, and metals such as gold. It wasn't until cutting and faceting became the norm that diamonds began appearing in more prominent sizes on royal jewelry. In fact, the first royal diamonds were reserved solely for the King as enacted by a law of Louis IX of France (1214–1270).

Diamond fashions really started to appear around 1600 when the gems took center stage away from metallic settings. Suddenly, the brilliance of gemstones became the focus of accessories, and gold or silver was merely a frame for their beauty. Ancient cuts like the rose, once again popular today, made their appearance as older cuts like the table and point cuts became outdated and simplistic.

It was during the eighteenth century that women took control of diamonds. In addition to Europe and India, diamonds were now being mined and shipped from South America, allowing more people the chance to own and wear them. A sign of social status, diamonds were worn by elegant ladies for the evening in matching sets—or *parures*—consisting of necklace, brooch, and earrings. South Africa's entry into the diamond game in the late 1800s once again completely changed the scope and availability of diamonds. Its Kimberley mines made diamonds a viable commodity. No longer reserved for only royalty or the fantastically wealthy, diamonds became a luxury available to any person who had the financial means to afford them.

So, when did the United States make it known that they would not be left behind in proving its diamond prowess? Ironically, it was with France's crown jewels. When Napoleon III's empire fell, France's magnificent collection of royal jewelry no longer had a place in government. When it was decided that the majority of it would be auctioned, it was assumed that much of it would be purchased by the major French players of the time such as Boucheron. But, when all was said and done, Tiffany & Co. of New York City walked away with twenty-two lots valued at nearly half a million dollars.

SPIRITUAL MATTERS

To some, the spiritual implications of diamonds far outweigh monetary ones. In the earliest known recordings that refer to diamonds, the healing properties of this stone are written of, in addition to its merely practical properties. An Indian legend stated that "[The diamond] overcomes and neutralizes poisons, dispels delirium, and banishes the groundless perturbations of the mind." In the sixth century text on gems by Buddha Bhatta called "Ratnapariksa," the manuscript specifically says: "He who wears [diamonds] will see dangers recede from him whether he be threatened by serpents, fire, poison, sickness, thieves, flood, or evil spirits."

In today's society, many gems are worn specifically to take advantage of their healing properties to the body and their benefits to the wearer. Diamonds, unsurprisingly, have been historically endowed with quite a few beneficial qualities ranging from the physical (balancing metabolism, clearing eyesight, strengthening the kidneys) to the mental (increasing creativity and bravery). According to the Diamond Information Center (DIC), there are five types of therapeutic diamonds. Colorless diamonds encourage love, balance, and purity. Black diamonds allow us to look inside ourselves honestly. Blue diamonds strengthen willpower. Pink diamonds foster creativity, and finally, yellow diamonds will help you be more thoughtful and considerate.

SPIRITUAL PROPERTIES OF GEMS

Yes, this book may be specifically about diamonds, but we can all probably use a little lift in our physical and spiritual selves. In addition to making us feel beautiful, our favorite gemstones may also contain additional benefits as we wear them. Here, directly from the Gemological Institute of America (GIA), are the alternative benefits of wearing rubies, emeralds, and sapphires.

- **EMERALD** A member of the beryl mineral species, emeralds contain chromium, which gives them their green color. In ancient Egypt, this tranquil green gem was highly prized by the wealthy and by priests. It is said that the Greek god Isis wore a green emerald in her headband and that those who looked upon it would be able to conceive. Emeralds in ancient Rome were highly prized and valued for their calming and soothing effects. Nero watched the Roman games in the Colosseum through a set of highly prized emerald glasses. Wearing emeralds, and almost all green gemstones, is thought to be advantageous for business/money ventures.

- **RUBY** Ruby is made of aluminum oxide (corundum). The red in rubies is caused by trace amounts of chromium—the redder the gem, the more chromium. The ruby represents the sun power in Hindu ancient writings and is said to have been given as an offering to Buddha in China and Krishna in India. An ancient belief about rubies was that dreaming of them meant the coming of success in money matters and love.

- **SAPPHIRE** Sapphire is also made of aluminum oxide and is considered the sister stone to the ruby. It comes in all colors except red, which has been designated as ruby. Buddhists believe that the sapphire favors devotion and spiritual enlightenment. The ancient Greeks linked sapphire with Apollo and wore it as an aid to prophecy when consulting oracles.

THE DIAMOND RIGHT-HAND RING

There has been no recent jewelry trend that speaks to the idea of female empowerment quite like the right-hand ring. A perfect symbol for today's successful, self-assured woman, this piece of jewelry suggests that a diamond ring is not only valuable when gifted by a man. So, how did this trend develop, and why are the most famous A-list celebrities all wearing their own symbols of empowerment?

The Diamond Trading Company (DTC) introduced the concept of the right-hand ring in 2003 with brilliant celebrity placements and a set of ads that celebrated independent women. All of a sudden stars like the women of the popular TV show, *Sex and the City* (Sarah Jessica Parker, Kristin Davis, Kim Cattral, and Cynthia Nixon), and singers/actresses Jennifer Lopez and Béyonce Knowles were all spotted on the red carpet with their right hands prominently displayed for the camera.

The concept was simple: women do not need a man to buy them a diamond ring, and, in fact, wearing one on your right hand not only expresses your independence but also your fash-

Right-hand rings are composed of clusters of diamonds with openings in the settings to allow skin to peek through.

ion savvy. This idea resonated with many types of women, including those who were not ready for marriage or hadn't yet found the right partner, those who had the financial means to purchase their own diamonds, and women who simply loved the look of diamonds but had previously stayed away because of the stigma that they should be a gift from a man.

The right-hand ring was positioned as a means of self-expression in the form of an accessory. According to the DTC, the right-hand ring is generally set in an open manner, allowing for the skin to peek through, in platinum or white gold with multiple diamonds of 0.20 carats or more. Four specific looks were pinpointed: Romantic, Modern Vintage, Floral, and Contemporary. Which style are you?

ROMANTIC ◆ Swirls and delicacy are hallmarks of Romantic right-hand rings. Relatively universal, these rings may incorporate elements of both the Modern Vintage and Floral.

"Romantic" right-hand ring by Caressa.

MODERN VINTAGE ◆ Do you love the look of antique jewelry and Old-World cuts? Then the Modern Vintage style of right-hand rings is probably for you. These rings often bear details like metal engraving and may even feature vintage cuts such as rose or Asscher.

"Modern Vintage" right-hand ring by Hearts on Fire.

FLORAL ♦ The name says it all: These rings are created with shapes that look like flowers. Sometimes, they are merely the representation of a flower shape and sometimes they are more realistic. Floral right-hand rings are a great way to incorporate colored diamonds into your look.

"Floral" right-hand ring by Fabrikant.

CONTEMPORARY ♦ This style reflects a sleek, modern appreciation for fashion. Less adorned and detailed than the other three looks, a contemporary right-hand ring is also often more geometric.

"Contemporary" right-hand ring by Daniel K.

ARE YOU A RIGHT-HAND RING WOMAN?

Here's the truth: There is a certain woman that the entire right-hand ring campaign was aimed at. Here's the demographic: She is a woman who has "likely been married at some point, received diamond jewelry before, and needs no one's permission to treat herself," according to the Diamond Trading Company. "She is proud of her own accomplishments and is evolved, savvy, and affluent." In addition, the target woman is 35 to 64 years old. This higher age range reflects women who are established and can afford their own jewelry.

Sound familiar? Then you might be just the person who can appreciate and understand the value of a right-hand ring. But, let's be clear: The only reason to buy yourself an expensive piece of jewelry is because you love it, and because it makes you feel good when you wear it. Don't buy into an ad campaign just because of a hot trend; make a purchase if it is the right decision for you.

Don't Break the Bank for a Right-Hand Ring

One fantastic benefit of the right-hand ring is its relatively affordable price points. Usually made up of smaller points of diamonds to create a sparkly effect, right-hand rings were created to be self-purchases and not something that you will have to take out a loan in order to afford. In fact, many famous jewelry designers have created their own versions of right-hand rings that sell for around $2,000.

If you're not ready to spend that much for the look of a right-hand ring, you can look to more affordable discount or superstores for their own versions. Often priced at around $300, these rings are usually lower-karat gold than what you would get from a major name designer, and the diamond quality might not be as good. No matter where you purchase your right-hand ring, always insist on a grading report to ensure authenticity.

Bling Is the Thing

Ever since the concept of the celebrity came about, stars have worn the world's most fabulous and expensive jewels. Whether it was a tactic to promote a specific jeweler or merely a testament to that celebrity's wealth and fame, the relationship between stars and gems has been a very friendly one. But now, as promoting jewelry at parties and on the red carpet becomes more and more *de rigeur* by Hollywood standards, the concept of "bling-bling" has come into its own, out of the shadows of rap and sports stars.

The term "bling bling" was coined in the late 1990s by the New Orleans rap family Cash Money Millionaires. One of its stars, Baby Gangsta (B.G.), brought the term to national awareness with his song "Bling Bling" that spoke of flashy diamonds and jewelry. While a slang term for years, bling went legit with its addition to the *Oxford English Dictionary* in 2003.

PROMOTING RIGHT-HAND RINGS

The Diamond Trading Company, an arm of the diamond giant, De Beers, sure knows how to make a statement. After inventing the slogan "A Diamond Is Forever" for engagement rings, the masterminds of diamond marketing came up with a persuasive campaign for their newest push, the right-hand ring. The ads, which were featured in all the top fashion and lifestyle magazines, featured catchy phrases that examine the differences between the right and left hand, and all the slogans ended with the statement: "Women of the world, raise your right hand." Here are a few examples of the copy featured in these successful ads:

- *Your left hand says "we." Your right hand says "me." Your left hand rocks the cradle. Your right hand rules the world.*

- *Your left hand lives for love. Your right hand lives for the moment. Your left hand wants to be held. Your right hand wants to be held high.*

- *Your left hand purrs. Your right hand pounces. Your left hand asks you "when." Your right hand tells you "now."*

So, you may be asking yourself, "Is this right-hand ring thing really a new concept?" Well, technically, any ring you may have worn on your right hand in the past that contained diamonds qualified. But the idea of empowering women to adorn themselves with diamonds was never really addressed before. Yes, there have always been those "ladies who lunch," who sport diamonds and gems from head to toe, but the right-hand ring phenomenon is hoping to open the door for all women to express their fashion tastes with diamond jewelry.

So, what exactly is bling and what are some examples of jewelry that fit the term? The word "bling" is used to describe diamonds, jewelry, and all forms of showy style and is often sported by high-profile rap and R&B artists, as well as super-star athletes, such as football and basketball players. These flashy celebs love to wear glittering, oversized medallions, huge diamond stud earrings, thick diamond bracelets, and encrusted rings. Some term the look as "iced out." But, you may be thinking, how does this affect me, and why would I want to sport bling? Well, bling has gone relatively main-stream in recent years. While übercelebs, such as Nicole Kidman and Renee Zellweger, may not be wearing enormous diamond-laden crucifixes or their names on huge diamond-encrusted medallions, they are literally dripping in diamonds at many high-profile events and award shows.

An illustration of a diamond-encrusted pendant by West Coat celebrity jeweler Chris Aire.

As jewelers aim to be more like fashion designers—having celebrities drop their brand name for the reporters—big stars are spending as much time on their accessories as they are on their gowns. Names such as Martin Katz, Harry Winston, and Neil Lane are becoming just as common as Gucci, Prada, and Chanel. This emphasis on jewels has had an effect at the consumer level as women are bejeweling themselves day and night, whether with brooches, chandelier earrings, or cocktail rings, to achieve the same glamorous look as their favorite stars.

So, how can you incorporate a little bling into your jewelry wardrobe? Here are a few tips for icing yourself out:

- ◆ Don't go overboard. Unless you have a top-ten hip-hop album on the charts or play for a pro basketball team, you probably won't want to accessorize with more than one or two flashy pieces. Let one over-the-top piece express your style—and your restraint.

- ◆ Invest in a piece that will sparkle and grab attention but that is not just trendy. Big solitaire diamond earrings are all the rage in bling circles but will also never go out of style.

- ◆ Another classic investment piece may be a watch that is dotted with diamonds. Look for styles that feature diamonds around the face of the watch for a look that is noticeable but not gaudy.

- ◆ To take a piece you already have from cool to bling, add more diamonds. For example, a diamond pendant on a plain metal chain can be updated with a chain that contains diamond chips. Diamonds by the Yard are long metal ropes that incorporate small diamonds. You can buy Diamonds by the Yard from many jewelry stores or wholesalers.

- ◆ Look for pieces that contain a lot of pavé or closely set diamonds. The overall effect will be one of glitter.
- ◆ Go for white on white pieces. Colorless diamonds and white metal make the most impact when hit by light.
- ◆ Have a piece custom made. If you can afford to work directly with a designer to create a one-of-a-kind piece, it can be your signature. Incorporate a symbol or icon that you love or that has meaning in your life. Look at it like a glittery tattoo: one that can be removed at your will!

GLOSSARY

AGS ✦ American Gem Society.

ART DECO ✦ Popular from about 1925–1940, a style of architecture and decoration characterized by abstract geometric shapes and bold colors.

ART NOUVEAU ✦ Popular in the late nineteenth and early twentieth centuries, a style of architecture and decoration characterized by floral motifs and flowing lines.

ASSCHER CUT ✦ The Asscher Diamond Company patented this rectilinear diamond cut in 1902. The deeply cut corners of its step cut give it an almost octagonal outline. Its features include a small table, a high crown, broad step facets, a deep pavilion, and a square culet.

BAGUETTE ✦ A style of step cutting for small, rectangular- or trapeze-shaped gemstones, principally diamonds.

BAR SETTING ✦ Often used in circular bands, the bar setting uses no prongs to hold the stones in place. Instead, the gems are separated by thin bars of metal.

BEZEL SETTING ✦ A setting in which a stone is held securely by a metal rim around the girdle.

BLING ✦ Slang for showy or ostentatious jewelry.

BRANDED DIAMOND ✦ A unique diamond cut marketed specifically by one vendor or retailer. A branded diamond is laser inscribed to certify its authenticity.

BRILLIANCE ✦ The reflection of white light that occurs when light moves through a diamond; sparkle.

BRILLIANT CUT ✦ Also referred to as *round-cut*, a cut of stone with a circular girdle that contains 57 or 58 facets, which gives off the maximum amount of light.

CARAT WEIGHT ✦ Equal to 0.200 g, the standard unit of weight for diamonds and most other gems.

CHANNEL SETTING ✦ A style of setting in which stones are set directly next to each other with no metal separation. Stones are held securely in place by two parallel metal rims.

CLARITY ✦ The measure of where a stone falls along the scale from flawless to imperfect. A clarity grade is determined by looking at the size, number, position, nature, and color of inclusions and blemishes internally and externally on a stone.

CLUSTER SETTING ✦ A setting in which a large gem is surrounded by several smaller gems.

COLORLESS DIAMONDS ✦ Classic, clear, "white" diamonds.

CONFLICT DIAMONDS ✦ Rough diamonds that are used by rebel movements to finance wars against legitimate governments.

CROWN ✦ The upper portion of a cut gemstone (from the *girdle* to the *table*).

CUBIC ZIRCONIA ✦ A common simulant, or imitation, of a natural diamond.

CULET ✦ The very small facet on the pointed bottom of a cut diamond.

DIAMETER ✦ The measurement of a gemstone across its widest part.

DIAMOND SIMULANT ✦ A solid substance created in the lab that imitates the appearance of a diamond.

DOUBLE-CLIP BROOCH ✦ Two identical clips that could be attached and worn as a single piece or worn separately; a style of jewelry popular during the Art Deco period.

EGL ✦ European Gemological Laboratory.

EMERALD CUT ✦ A rectangular cut of gemstone with truncated corners; this style has fewer facets overall than most cuts.

ENAMELING ✦ A decorative technique that involves fusing glass to metal with high heat.

FACET ✦ Any flat, polished surface of a gemstone. The number of facets in a stone varies by style of cut and the stone's dimensions.

FANCY COLORED DIAMONDS ✦ Any diamond with a strong, naturally occurring color. Reddish, blue, and green are very rare; orange and violet, rare; strong yellow, yellowish-green brown, and black stones are more common.

FOUR C'S ✦ A popular phrase in diamond evaluation that refers to Color, Cut, Clarity, and Carat weight.

FIRE ✦ The reflection of rainbow colors off the facets that occurs when light moves through a diamond.

FLAT-TOP SETTING ✦ A setting of gemstone that features a band that is thicker, broader and flattened at the top, and relies on clips to set the stone securely; related to the *gypsy setting*.

FLAWLESS ✦ A measure of clarity given to a stone that shows no inclusions or blemishes under 10x magnification.

FRACTURE FILLING ✦ A technique that uses a molten, glasslike substance to fill a break or chip in a stone.

GIA ✦ Gemological Institute of America.

GIRDLE ✦ The rim (or circumference) of a cut gemstone.

GYPSY SETTING ✦ A style of stone setting that features one continuous band that comes to a thicker, dome shape at the top of the ring. The gem is then set within this dome, creating a smooth, clean look.

HEART CUT ✦ A heart-shaped variation of the brilliant cut that originates from a pear shape. The round end of the pear is flattened and notched, and the girdle widened until the length of the heart is approximately equal to its width.

HPHT TREATMENT ✦ An initialism for "high pressure, high temperature" treatment; a method for creating synthetic diamonds.

IGI ✦ International Gemological Institute.

INCLUSION ✦ A small, internal flaw or crack in a diamond.

JA ✦ Jewelers of America.

JVC ✦ Jewelers Vigilance Committee.

INDEPENDENT RETAILERS ✦ Stores not tied to national chains. Sometimes known as mom-and-pop stores.

KARAT ✦ A unit of measure denoting the purity of gold; pure gold is 24 karat.

KIMBERLEY PROCESS ✦ A joint initiative between governments, the international diamond industry, and civil society to stem the flow of conflict diamonds into the market.

LASER DRILLING ✦ Used to remove inclusions permanently, laser drilling relies on a tiny laser beam to tunnel into a stone. The marks left by laser drilling often look more natural than those that are fracture filled.

MARQUISE CUT ✦ A cut of gem in an elliptical shape with pointed ends.

MOISSANITE ♦ A simulant diamond produced by Charles & Colvard.

OLD MINE ♦ An early form of brilliant cut with a squarelike, but rounded, girdle outline; also known as *cushion*.

OVAL CUT ♦ A brilliant style of cut gem in which the girdle outline is elliptical.

PAVÉ SETTING ♦ A setting of gemstone in which one prong comes into contact with at least three stones; similar to the *channel setting*.

PAVILION ♦ The lower portion of a cut gemstone (from the girdle to the culet).

PEAR-SHAPE CUT ♦ A cut diamond with a girdle outline in the shape of a tear drop.

PGS ♦ Professional Gem Services.

POLISH ♦ The relative smoothness of a surface, or the degree to which the finish of the surface approaches optical perfection.

PRINCESS CUT ♦ A modern, square-cut gem with extra faceting along the rim for added brilliance.

PRONG SETTING ♦ A setting in which the stone is held in place with claws, or prongs, allowing light to shine through the bottom of the stone; the most common setting for a diamond.

RADIANT CUT ♦ A rectangular cut of gem with extra facets on the bottom of the stone; this cut is particularly sparkly, as the name implies.

RIGHT-HAND RING ♦ A jewelry style promoted by the Diamond Trading Company; the marketing campaign encourages women to wear diamonds on their right hand as a symbol of independence and empowerment.

ROSE CUT ✦ A cut of gem with a flat, unfaceted base and a dome-shaped top formed by a number of triangular facets that terminate in a point. The number of facets varies by the size of the gem.

ROUND CUT ✦ See *brilliant cut*.

SAUTOIR ✦ A long necklace, popular during the Art Deco period, containing strong geometric shapes and versatile, often detachable, components that could be used as additional pieces of jewelry.

SCINTILLATION ✦ The flash achieved when light bounces between the facets on a stone.

SOLITAIRE ✦ A ring or earring that features only one stone.

SYMMETRY ✦ Balanced proportions between halves of an object. The more symmetrical a diamond's cut is, the more fire and brilliance (or sparkle) will be achieved.

SYNTHETIC DIAMONDS ✦ A manmade gemlike material with essentially the same physical, optical, and chemical properties as diamonds; similar to *diamond simulant*.

TABLE FACET ✦ The top facet of a gemstone, which is the largest facet of the stone.

TABLE PERCENTAGE ✦ A comparison of the width of the table facet and the width of the girdle expressed as a percentage.

TENSION SETTING ✦ A setting in which the gem is held in place solely by pressure from the band.

TOTAL DEPTH ✦ The height of a gemstone as measured from the culet to the table.

TRILLION ✦ A stone that is cut and shaped into a triangle; often set to flank a center stone.

Resources

Designers and Retailers

Alan Bronstein/Aurora Gems
589 Fifth Avenue
New York, NY 10017 USA
212-355-1480
www.auroragems.com

Beaverbrooks
44-0800-169-2329
www.beaverbrooks.co.uk
contact for all locations

Bulgari US Flagship
730 Fifth Avenue
New York, NY 10019 USA
212-315-9000
www.bulgari.com
contact for all locations

Cartier
653 Fifth Avenue
New York, NY 10022 USA
800-227-8437
www.cartier.com
contact for all locations

Charles & Colvard Created
    Moissanite, Ltd.
300 Perimeter Park, Suite A
Morrisville, NC 27560 USA
919-468-0399
800-210-4367 (toll free)
www.moissanite.com

Chris Aire/ 2 Awesome
    International
P.O. Box 811726
Los Angeles, CA 90081 USA
877-500-AIRE (2743)
213-688-0900
www.2awesomeint.com

Costco
800-774-2678
www.costco.com
contact for all locations

De Beers
www.debeers.com

Diamond Information Center/
Diamond Trading Company
www.adiamondisforever.com

eBay
www.ebay.com

Ernest Jones
44-0800-389-5952
www.ernestjones.co.uk
contact for all locations

F Hinds
44-0800-034-4637
www.fhinds.co.uk
contact for all locations

Goldsmiths
44-0116-232-2200 (fax)
www.goldsmiths.co.uk
contact for all locations

H Samuel
44-0800-389-4683
www.hsamuel.co.uk
contact for all locations

Half Price Jewelers
44-0870-606-4655
www.hpj-jewelers.co.uk
contact for all locations

Harry Winston
718 Fifth Avenue
New York, NY 10019 USA
212-245-2000
www.harrywinston.com
contact for all locations

Home Shopping Network
800-933-2887
www.hsn.com

Jewelry Television/Comcast
865-692-6100
www.jewelrytelevision.com

Martin Katz, Ltd.
310-276-7200 (Los Angeles)
212-957-8295 (New York)
www.martinkatz.com

Neil Lane
8840 Beverly Boulevard
Los Angeles, CA 90048 USA
310-275-5015
www.neillanejewelry.com

QVC
888-345-5788
www.qvc.com

Robert Lee Morris
400 West Broadway
New York, NY 10012 USA
212-431-9305
www.robertleemorris.com

Stephen Webster–USA
317 Madison Avenue, Suite 1119
New York, NY 10017 USA
212-226-6160
www.stephenwebster.com

Stephen Webster–London
75 Gloucester Place
London W1U 8JP UK
44-0-20-7486-6576

Tiffany & Co.
Fifth Avenue at 57th Street
New York, NY 10022 USA
212-755-8000
www.tiffany.com
contact for all locations

Van Cleef & Arpels
744 Fifth Avenue
New York, NY 10019 USA
212-644-9500
www.vancleef.com
contact for all locations

Vera Wang Flagship Salon
653 Fifth Avenue
New York, NY 10022 USA
800-VEW-VERA
www.verawang.com
contact for all locations

Wal-Mart
800-925-6278
www.walmart.com
contact for all locations

Warren James
www.warrenjames.co.uk
contact for all locations

Zale Corp.
Zales
800-311-5393
www.zales.com
Gordons
888-467-3661
Bailey Banks & Biddle
800-651-4222
Piercing Pagoda
800-866-9700
Peoples
800-211-2272
Mappins
800-519-4653
Zales Outlet
800-950-4367

Industry Organizations

American Gem Society (AGS)
8881 West Sahara Avenue
Las Vegas, NV 89117 USA
702-255-6500
www.ags.org

Association for Contemporary
Jewellery (UK)
44-020-8291-4201
enquiries@acj.org.uk

Auction Market Research/Gail
Brett Levine. GG
P.O. Box 7683
Rego Park, NY 11374-7683 USA
718-897-7305
76766.614@compuserve.com

Better Business Bureau
703-276-0100
www.bbb.com
contact for all locations

British Antique Dealers'
Association
44-020-8291-4201

British Jewellers' Association
44-0121-236-2657

Consumer Direct (UK)
44-08454-04-05-06
www.consumerdirect.gov.uk

European Gemological
Laboratory–USA (EGL)
6 West 48th Street
New York, NY 10036 USA
212-730-7380
www.eglusa.com

Federal Trade Commission
www.ftc.gov

Gemological Institute of America
(GIA)
World Headquarters
The Robert Mouawad Campus
5345 Armada Drive
Carlsbad, CA 92008 USA
800-421-7250
760-603-4000 (outside U.S. and
Canada)
www.gia.edu

Irish Jewellers Association
353-1-296-0920
www.irish-jewellers-association.com

International Gemological
Institute–USA (IGI)
589 Fifth Avenue
New York, NY 10017 USA
212-753-7100
www.igi-usa.com

International Titanium Association
2655 West Midway Boulevard
Suite 300
Broomfield, CO 80020-7186 USA
303-404-2221
www.titanium.org

JCRS
3345 Grand Avenue, Suite 4
Oakland, CA 94610 USA
510-444-4811
www.jcrs.com

Jewelers of America (JA)
52 Vanderbilt Avenue, 19th Floor
New York, NY 10017 USA
646-658-0246
www.jewelers.org

Jewelers Vigilance Committee
25 West 45th Street
Suite 400
New York, NY 10036 USA
212-997-2002
www.jvclegal.org

Jewellery Distributors'
    Association UK
Federation House
10 Vyse Street
Birmingham, B18 4BR UK
44-0845-2260-532
www.jda.org.uk
secretariat@jda.org.uk

Jewelry Information Center
52 Vanderbilt Avenue, 19th Floor
New York, NY 10017 USA
800-459-0130
www.jic.org

Platinum Guild International–USA
www.preciousplatinum.com

The Silver Institute
1200 G Street, NW
Suite 800
Washington, DC 20005 USA
202-835-0185
www.silverinstitute.org

TrustUK
DMA House
70, Margaret Street
London, W1W 8SS UK
44-020-7291-3345
www.trustuk.org.uk

World Gold Council–Europe
(WGC)
55 Old Broad Street
London EC2M 1RX UK
44-0-20-7826-4700

World Gold Council–USA (WGC)
444 Madison Avenue
New York, NY 10022 USA
212-317-3800
www.gold.org

INDUSTRY NEWS PUBLICATIONS

Jewelers Circular Keystone
    Magazine
360 Park Avenue South
New York, NY 10010 USA
www.jckgroup.com

JQ Magazine
585 Fifth Street West
Sonoma, CA 95476 USA
707-938-1082
www.retailmerchandising.net

Modern Jeweler/Lustre Magazines
3 Huntington Quadrangle
Suite 301N
Melville, NY 11747 USA
631-845-2700
www.modernjeweler.com

National Jeweler Magazine
770 Broadway, 5th Floor
New York, NY 10003 USA
646-654-4926
www.nationaljeweler.com

Professional Jeweler Magazine
1500 Walnut Street
Suite 1200
Philadelphia, PA 19102 USA
888-557-0727
www.professionaljeweler.com

Rapaport Diamond Report
702-893-9600
www.diamonds.net

Index

Photography and Illustration Credits

Boccia/www.boccia.com, 53
Courtesy of Alan Bronstein/Robert Weldon, 28 (center)
Courtesy of Alan Bronstein/Tino Hammid, 27, 28 (top, bottom), 29, 30
Caressa by Design Works, 115
Charles & Colvard/www.moissanite.com, 36
Daniel K./www.danielk.net, 116
Fabrikant/www.fabrikant.com, 116
Courtesy of Gemological Institute of America, 38
Hearts on Fire/www.heartsonfire.com, 115
Kwiat/www.kwiat.com, 114
Courtesy of Jewelers of America, 87
Courtesy of Jewelers Vigilance Committee, 88
Robert Lee Morris/www.robertleemorris.com, 59

Tacori/www.tacori.com, 52
Courtesy of Tiffany & Co., 6
Courtesy of Tiffany & Co./Carlton Davis, 3, 40, 80
Courtesy of Tiffany & Co./Richard Pierce, 16, 64, 74, 106
Courtesy of Tiffany & Co./Stephen Lewis, 12
Stephen Webster, 61, 74
Courtesy of World Gold Council/Gregor Halenda, 48, 49, 50, 51

All illustrations are by Robyn Neild, except those appearing on page 35, which are by Chuck Lockhart.

ABOUT THE AUTHOR

Younga Park

After receiving her degree in Print Journalism from James Madison University, Randi Molofsky embarked on her jewelry career with a position as the Fashion Editor at the biweekly *National Jeweler*. Through the coverage of international and domestic trade shows, as well as innumerable visits to designers and trade associations, she became a respected figure in the jewelry community.

A busy schedule of judging major design competitions and speaking on panels at the Fashion Institute of Technology and the Learning Annex, among others, has kept this New York City–based jewelry consultant at the forefront of the field. A committee chair for the Women's Jewelry Association, Randi started a jewelry consulting firm, moodring, in 2003. In addition to freelancing for magazines including *W Jewelry*, *Jewelry Connoisseur*, and *Couture International Jeweler*, she has placed jewels on major celebrities for award shows and has been featured on television as a jewelry expert.

ACKNOWLEDGMENTS

Many thanks to Hedda Schupak for the recommendation; thehappycorp for the shelter and support; The Diamond Information Center, World Gold Council, Platinum Guild International, Gemological Institute of America, and Jewelry Information Center for valuable resources and materials; Alan Bronstein, Stephen Webster, and Robert Lee Morris; Donna Frishknecht for my first jewelry job; my editor Delilah Smittle for her unending patience and good spirit; and, last but certainly not least, the thousands of jewelers I've met from across the globe who continue to enchant me with their fabulous art.